RENE

MW01226012

MOST
WANTED
...a true story of change

Library and Archives Canada Cataloguing in Publication
Durocher, Rene
Most Wanted: a true story of change/ Rene Durocher
ISBN: 978-0-9731557-9-2
Most Wanted: a true story of change
Copyright@ 2019 by Rene Durocher

To protect identities, I have changed some names.

Net profits from this book will be donated to The Winnipeg Foundation in support of programs that resource victims of serious crime.

For more information contact:
Rene Durocher
durocher.r@icloud.com
204.963.1702

Dedicated to my wife,
my children, their partners and my grandchildren

CONTENTS

Preface

When I was diagnosed with fibromyalgia, it was a shock for me to find out that I am not superman. It is the worst shock I've had in a long time. When the doctor told me this in his office, I told him to go fuck himself.

When he wanted to give me a prescription, I said, "Stick it."

Imagine, I was 72 years old – and I still believed I was superhuman.

That's how I have been all my life. When doing crimes or working with Life Line or whatever, I was always a superman – a guy who can never be stopped. I grew up like that.

When my partner was killed, it nearly did me in, but I bit the bullet and persevered the best way I knew.

I had always been an extremist. I had to be superhuman to do the work that I did with inmates. People were always saying, "Rene, slow down. You'll go crazy."

I would reply, "No, I have things to do." For me, it was never work. My job was like a mission – a passion. I knew I could make a difference. I wanted to make a difference for the guys who were not real offenders.

Why would they stop when they get back on the streets? That's what the government didn't understand. In jail we are trained to survive, and when we get out and go back on the streets, we have to use the same skills to survive. Superhumans cannot be weak.

This never changed.

When I changed from a criminal to a father, I used all my extreme energy for the battle of good. I was motivated to the extreme. I wanted to help, to make a difference.

You cannot change a human being. You can change his values and his actions in life, but you cannot change his character – the person he has been. I was still the same human being except my passion had changed.

When I was diagnosed with fibromyalgia, I felt I was finished. I felt it was time to go.

I looked at my age and saw that I was becoming like a vegetable. How could I live like that?

Fibromyalgia takes away your energy. I didn't have the energy to go out and speak anymore. Every nerve ending screaming with pain probably because of the life I had lived.

I stood at the riverside – not the gentle Red River but the Sturgeon Creek which is a rather innocent-looking, insignificant creek but it has this insidious undercurrent. I knew that if I plunged into this creek that was really a river, I would not have a chance for a second thought.

I knew that there would be no chance for me to come back. Oh my god, Sturgeon Creek is so powerful. It's the most dangerous area in Winnipeg for drowning. I had studied everything carefully. I didn't choose the Red River because I would have had to jump off a bridge to die. It's not deep enough at the edge. If you jump close to the bridge, you're gone. You cannot make it. I just drove to Sturgeon Creek that night. When I was in that state of mind, the car went there automatically.

But something kept me from entering those waters that day. There is something that has kept me alive…. I should have died a million times – but I didn't.

Why? I've asked that a million times. My conclusion - I think I was meant to write this book - an examination of a wild and crazy life that I have lived. So - I'm going to try to put it together for you – some of the details might have escaped me but this is how I remember it.

Present situation

Suzanne and I are doing well now. We manage to laugh a lot. We spent the weekend painting, even if I can't do too much. I painted one wall in the kitchen, and one in the living room. We do things together and you learn to appreciate being with that person.

I try to teach my grandson. My grandson is brilliant – not because he is my grandson. He is really brilliant. He is always with adults. Now he has a sister.

I now have the will to live for my grandkids. I am reliving what I missed. Last time I was arrested, my daughter was two, and my son was four. I missed five years of being with them. Now I have two grandchildren.

I am so proud that I am their grandpa. It is not the other way around. I am so proud that I was lucky enough to meet this boy and this girl.

My grandson has already given me back the will to live. It is crazy. When I wanted to leave and jump into the river, my daughter said, "You always asked me to give you grandkids. Now you have them and you want to leave?"

That really opened my eyes. That gives me the will to live. I just hope I can live so both of them remember who papi is.

My granddaughter is like an angel, she is so beautiful. We spend a lot of time with them. All last week we babysat because Mel had so much running around to do to prepare for her trip. We spend a lot of time with them, even when we are tired. You get tired when you are running around after them. Oh my god, but you miss them when they are gone.

They are part of your life - like doing things with my grandson. He's a bundle of energy compared to me. That is what he gives me.

He shows me I am not superman. He shows me love.

CHAPTER ONE
Knife Slipped

I was a young boy when a priest came to our house. He told my mother that I had great potential. He said that I would become a great person someday.

He just wasn't sure whether it would be a great prime minister – or a great criminal.

I chose to become a great criminal.

And I was one of the best.

It was what I was destined for – it was what life groomed me for.

It was my model – my father was violent.

Until I was five years old, I didn't even know who my father was or what that word even meant. You don't know a father who hasn't been around, who has never taken you into his arms or put you to bed.

He had actually left my mother way before I was born. I think he was coming home to see the children, or whatever, and then they would end up in bed, and she would have another baby. This was his history. He would come home, use our mother and…and never really stayed to be a father to the children. It was a love-hate relationship. It was what my mother had for him. Conflicted.

My few memories I have of him was of their constant fighting. I couldn't understand the tension at the time. Now I understand. My father had made a life with another woman, and I don't know how many children he had with her so when he did come, there was tension. I'm left with the early memories of the endless fighting in the house. My mother always said she hated him.

My most vivid memory – that still sticks with me – is the time the argument turned into violence. I can still see – vividly – my father picking up a knife and lunging at my mom to stab her. She ducked and the blade hit the wall. When his hand hit the wall, the knife slipped and he sliced his hand – cutting all the tendons in his fingers. He was yelling, she was screaming, and all I remember is that from that day on, I can only see the blood, hear the screaming. It never left me.

I hated my father from that day on. I hated him with a passion.

The slash, the blood, the scream… that is what sticks with me to this day.

As a child, one of the first things, my most vivid memory is of that knife going into the wall, and you don't know how to take it. I imagine my mother took me in her arms to try to comfort me but…. I don't know what my father did. He probably left right away. I know that the screaming stopped. There was blood on the floor and the wall, but there was no more screaming between the two of them. That one scene affected me. I hated my father ever after – and I wanted revenge.

A year and a half later, when I was at the convent, he came to visit us – my sister and me. He had changed. I was surprised at the sight of him. He had a moustache. He wasn't the huge man I remember; he was only a little bit taller than I was. It was like he was a stranger and I was meeting a stranger. The only way that I was certain it was my father, was when I saw his hand. It was deformed. He was not able to close his hand. When you are a kid, you forget the face of the person and stuff like this, so it was a shock to see him – and see that his hand had closed permanently.

I spoke to him for two seconds, just long enough to tell him that I never wanted to see him again.

Even just the sound of his name brought out the rage in me. The next time I heard about him was when I was at my mother's place and one of my sisters came home and told my mother that she had seen my father walking down the street. I just ran out of the house, slamming the door behind and went to look for him. I just wanted to beat the shit out of him. Even just the mention of his name would send me into a fit of rage.

I never found him. Glad I didn't.

I always told myself that I would never be like him. I always saw the bad part of my father – never the good part. I am sure he had a good part… but I never saw it. I just was filled with hate – and this deep void for a father figure. All I could think of was beating the shit out of my father – for letting me down – moving out of my life – never giving me any father model to live by – no support. I truly disowned him.

My mother failed me too... or at least that is the conclusion I came to. She couldn't provide for us as children. After my father's bloody assault, my mother went to work at a place where they were killing chickens, as well as an assistant nurse at the hospital. She worked two jobs.

Oh my god, she had to work hard!

To survive it all, she became a kind of dictator. We had to do what she wanted or we would get it. No doubt. She wanted to control everything! She was a control freak. I guess she didn't know any better.

Then it went from bad to worse. Shortly after that event my mother was diagnosed with cancer. They gave her six months to live. She had a bag on her side for the rest of her life. She was bitter, she was angry. She had no choice but to place us in care.

I was six years old when all the children in our family were split up and placed in different places. Since there were no agencies, my mother placed us all through a nearby convent. I was placed in a Catholic foster home.

I had no say. I don't remember any discussion over it. I just recall being told that I was going, and them saying, okay we are going to place you there.

She took us back when she could. But we were so poor – we could hardly exist. I remember one time when I was particularly upset with my mother, I ran away for the first time. I don't know how I did it. You are so young, you fight against the world but you don't know why. What can you do when you are so young, you just don't know? It is just later that you start to make sense of it. I was so angry and hurt, I became quite aggressive toward these people after that.

It was only for a few days that first time. I don't know how long I spent, maybe a day or two, I don't know. After that, I was running away and coming back in two days. She hardly noticed my coming and going. She had another four-five-six mouths to feed at home. She had nine children in total and if one isn't there, one less mouth to feed. I would escape to a tram, sometimes spent the night on the go. It is like that…when you have a fear to go back, you find anything that will help you to survive. Even she was surviving, she had so much that it was a relief when I wasn't there. It is for that – that I left home so early.

I was just a rebellious kid after that… I didn't do well in school.

I didn't learn anything. I know that they always told me, "You are so smart, why are you like this?" "You are so smart why do you do that?" and I know I was smart, but I was using my smarts right then to protect myself. I didn't need to study; I was getting all my education in a different way. I didn't want to take the book, I didn't want to do anything, I was just smart kid, I don't doubt in my mind.

I know I was smart. You learn that quickly when you start to fear everybody. I was smart for the wrong reason. When everybody is afraid of you. "You see I am smarter than you, now you are going to have to do what I am telling you and get away from me."

I was a dictator just as my mom was, she was a dictator and I was a dictator.

I wanted to live my life like I wanted to, and no one was going to tell me what I am going to do. I think by twelve I was smacking people over the head. In Quebec, every park had signs stuck in the ground with a rebar post, which was flat – about half of an inch thick and about three feet long. At the top of the post, there was attached a little piece of wood that would say, "Don't walk on the grass." And every park had those signs in those days. I was taking one out of the ground and when I saw someone, I would just smack them for no reason, just to look for a fight, just to get my anger out of me.

CHAPTER TWO
Predator

I was sexually assaulted when I was a kid…. That's why I hate sex offenders.

After my father's bloody assault, my mother went to work. Nothing worked out and I was put into foster care. That's when I started to attend church.

Every kid at six or seven years old was formally introduced into the church by baptism, communion and confirmation. As an altar boy, you can help serve communion in the church. There was mass every morning – and I was always ready to serve.

I loved to go to church. I can still remember my First Communion by the Bishop.

I had my First Communion in a private chapel. That's when the Monseigneur said that I would either be a brilliant statesman or a great criminal. I still remember that. It was in my head all the time, even as I was choosing to be a criminal. I remembered that he said I would be "great."

I liked mass. It was a ritual that I could count on. It felt comfortable.

At that time, the priests were very involved in the day-to-day activity of their parishioners. They would visit every family – often controlling them.

Back then they were telling the families to have more children. They prohibited contraception and taught that sex was designed only to have children. And the people obeyed and had children.

So I was taught to believe that the priest was a voice from God, and someone who could not do anything wrong. I truly believed that they were the best people in the world, because that is the way they were introduced to me.

And that is where the nightmare happened in my life.

I have never spoken about this before – not to anybody. The first time I was sexually assaulted was when I was seven. It was by the priest after I had made my First Communion.

We were in the back preparing for mass – when he pulled me aside and touched me. Then he made me touch him, then he took me in his mouth.

When you are a kid – only seven years old – you don't even know what this means. You don't have a clue, you just freeze, and you cannot talk to no one because it is the priest.

In those years in Quebec, the priests were revered like no one else. They were in control – they ruled everything.

Very carefully, he aroused me – sexualized me – and played me.

I saw him every day, so he had his way with me every day – and I could not tell the family I lived with.

That priest did that for about six to eight months, almost daily. After a while, I was living it. There is nothing you can say; you just scream and cry.

I am sure that he did this to all the other kids, but we never talked. We were taught to be very secretive, don't say a word and it is OK. It is religion. They can brainwash you with anything because they are used to preaching, and all that stuff. Then they can take you for the ride of your life, and you don't ever know you are taking the ride of your life.

You get to the point where you feel you are responsible for it. I was a cute kid… even a "good-looking kid," and I was more vulnerable because he was attracted to me. But I didn't know that it was him and his choosing me – I just felt guilty. It was my key secret, for me.

It should have been the other way around. He should have carried the guilt of it – but he didn't. I did. I shouldn't have even seen him as a priest – he was a sexual predator. Sexual predators have a way of attracting children. You put a sexual predator in a robe, then you believe that he is god, and you haven't a clue what he is doing to you…not only physically but emotionally as well. When you grow up, it affects you in ways you would never guess.

I dealt with it the only way I could. I began to act out. I just lost it. I became violent.

I did everything you can do to get kicked out of that foster family's home. I fought with them, threw things at them, and never wanted to sleep. When it was time to sleep, I was running away. I gave hell to these people – who were strictly good people that wanted to help a kid. But the kid doesn't understand that. When everything you see in your life is violence, you can't tell these people – good people – that you have been sexually assaulted.

Finally, that family was not able to take it anymore, and they sent me away.

Then I was sent into a convent run by the Grey Nuns on Cote de Liesse – a kind of residential school for French children.

I acted out my anger there too.

I wanted them to be afraid of me, and I was successful at this. Because I was so violent even the ones I had never touched were afraid. Everyone was afraid of a guy like me, because when I was losing it, you can see in my eyes that "this guy is going to kill me." My violence was extreme. It is what I saw the first time in my life, extreme violence.

I was a dictator. I wanted control. I hit people almost daily. I called down everyone, the teachers – everyone. When I fought, I would use my feet and my hands. You learn to survive on the street. I kicked... when you fight, you do that, because a swift kick to the groin, it hurts, and you are in control.

I wanted to be the macho guy there – every day. When they were afraid of me, they would not harm me. I was the guy they were afraid of, and it was my goal to keep that status, because when you make people afraid of you, they don't attack you.

And it was self-defense for me, with that same picture.

I was extremely violent. You live with that violence, because you don't know anything else, and you feel rejected by everybody. Then I kept running away, and running away from school.

I think it's because I never felt valuable. I never felt anything those days, never. I always felt like an object. I've always felt that hatred for others because I felt their hatred for me. For me it is like my heart turned into a heart of stone.

Everything a kid can do for no reason at all, I was doing it. It was my self-defense, and I grew up like this, and I was still like this for years and years.

When you fight and you fight, you get good at it, and when you throw the first punch, the guys go down, because you fight so often, and I was good at it.

I was a righty and I was hitting harder with my left. It is kind of funny, because I am ambidextrous with anything I do. When I played baseball, I hit on both sides of the plate. In hockey I am a lefty. I was hitting them and they didn't expect a left coming from a righty.

You become smarter because it is survival. There were other kids that wanted to be like me, but they could not overtake me because I was losing it.

Sometimes I was doing things I didn't even know I was doing. I was in a zone where everybody there was against me.

I was just angry at the world. And when you are angry like that you take your anger out on anyone -- even on Sister Caya that I thought was an angel! Some of the nuns were good. But I think I felt anger towards her as well. But even though I wasn't always nice to her – she didn't react to me. She was so nice. Every night she was being like a mom to me. She would come to my bed, tuck me in, and give me a kiss on the forehead, and said, "Good night." How can you do that? But no other nun ever did that, just Sister Caya.

The second sexual assault happened when I was living at home, still on De la Naudiere Street. I was about 12 at this time. My mother had managed to get her life together, collected all her children, and we were living at home.

My mother had a friend, Father Dufresne. I don't know his first name. I cannot remember ever calling him by his first name. I found out later that he had been a priest in the Catholic Church and had been defrocked. He travelled all over Quebec selling hair growth products – something that was popular in the mid-50s.

At one point he asked my mother, "Would you mind if I take one of your sons with me for two or three days?"

This would be a huge savings for my mother – to have one less mouth to feed for a few days.

I went with him to remote places on one of these trips – 400 or 500 miles away from home. It was winter – terrible conditions. The snowbanks were 20 feet high on both sides of the road. When we got to the first house and rang the bell, the man let us in. He knew the priest because he had bought products from him before. And we sometimes would stay the night. I think there were two bedrooms, but we ended up in the same bedroom. I was naive. I guess I hadn't learned yet. That was when I was sexually assaulted the second time.

It was brutal. He assaulted me like a son of a bitch. He started by taking me in his mouth and then he tried to get his penis inside me. It didn't work. I was mad. I was crying but I couldn't run away. It was the middle of winter and I only had an old jacket. I didn't own many clothes back then. We were in the middle of nowhere. Even if I had run, I would probably have died from exposure in an hour or two.

When I got back to the city after the trip, I didn't even go into the house. I ran away. I didn't want to be questioned. I didn't want to be asked anything. I was afraid.

I was angry with my mother because she was the one who was instrumental in pushing me into the relationship with the priest. When kids come home, they usually say, "Mom!" but I never did that. I always stood up to her. None of my siblings did. That's why I left home at such a young age. I was a rebellious kid. I wanted to live my own life. Nobody was going to tell me what I could do and where I could go. No one could stop me now.

Actually, I don't think my mother knew about the sexual assaults. I never talked to her about it. But I blamed her.

It all came out – this hatred for priests – at another time when my mother had cancer and was really sick. One day I saw my brother and he said, "Mom is sick."

We didn't know what to do.

I went to see her at home. I was about 14 at this time. My brother tried to get her to the hospital, but she didn't want to go. She said, "I don't want to go to the hospital. I want to stay here, here, here!"

Then someone called the priest.

As soon as the priest came into the house, I went to the kitchen. I didn't want to have anything to do with him, but I heard him tell my brother and sister, "If your mother dies, it will be your fault because you don't want her to go to the hospital."

I went into the room and said, "Get the fuck out of here!" I called him every name in the book. I said, "Don't ever come into this house again because I'll fuckin' throw you out!" I wanted to beat him up. I exploded. It's as if my non-communication and communication with them over the years exploded.

That is the last time in my life that I spoke to a priest.

CHAPTER THREE
Handgun

I got my first handgun when I was 13 years old. I paid $50, maybe $100 for the gun – money from small shoplifting that I had been doing. Then I started pulling armed robberies in the corner stores.

After I bought the gun, me and the guys would go out into the woods to practice. To shoot, you had to know your gun, be able to load it quickly. We would practice shooting at birds and trees. I learned to know my gun very well.

Every time I pointed the gun at someone, I felt the power. It was like being a race car driver with the best car in the world.

Owning a gun was a rush!

And then there was my switchblade knife. I'd stick it into my waistband – easy to grab with my right hand. Even if it was invisible, everyone knew it was there. And nobody wanted to approach you! No one in the neighborhood could say that I was a chicken. I was not afraid of anyone or anything.

My life was full of hate. My gun became the extension of my violence, my hatred. I didn't only feel it; I made a point of exuding hatred. I really worked at my image. Everything I did, the way I talked, the way I walked, even the way I dressed, all said, "Don't approach me."

When I started doing robberies, I met a guy who was almost as daring and crazy as I was. He was older, yet I took the lead. I was the brave, macho kid so I just told him, "Hey, follow me," and he did. We were the perfect team.

I was happy when people hated me. If they hated me, it meant that they were afraid of me. Violence attracted me.

I was only 14 when my sister, who was singing at a nightclub, needed a bouncer so I volunteered to be her bouncer. I just sat there, listening to her. She sounded like Doris Day. I didn't drink. I didn't like booze even back then.

I would put my gun on the table and watch. If there was trouble, I would say, "You have two choices. You are leaving …or else." If I told the guy to lie down on the floor, he would. All I would say is, "If you don't, I will shoot you." I felt so powerful watching over my older sister and taking care of her. In the end, I didn't shoot anyone. It was all just threats – but it worked. Everyone called me "Mister."

At 14 years of age I started wearing stocking masks to do the robberies. No one could recognize me because the stocking flattens your nose, your face. People were afraid of me. I wasn't a nervous kid. I would say, "Get down. Open the till." People would freeze from fear.

After the till is open, taking the money is the easy part. I would just take the big bills – $5, $10, $20. There weren't many $100 bills in the corner stores.

The quicker you get in, the quicker you get out. I did most of the robberies by myself at that point.

I ended up in a flat with a 21-year-old girl who was already pregnant. She wasn't my girlfriend – just another person who needed a place to live. We had sex a few times but it was boring for me to be with her in the apartment. I didn't stay with her very long. I even left some of my clothes in the apartment and didn't bother to get them back. If you had $100 back then, it was like being a millionaire. It was amazing.

The first thing I bought with the money was a pair of jeans to look like Elvis.

Elvis Presley was the top singer of the world. He was the greatest idol in the 50s. There was nothing cooler than Elvis. I tried to go into the army like him but I wasn't accepted. They probably realized that I wasn't cut out to be a soldier.

I was so cool – in leather jacket, jeans and boots with spurs - and my Elvis Presley haircut. He was my hero. It was his music that attracted me and his movie when he was tough. In most of his movies, he always had fights.

I also liked to look at pictures of Marilyn Monroe and go the movies. There was a theatre on Mont Royal Street. On Sunday afternoons, you could see three movies for 50 cents.

I would pick an Elvis movie or a Grace Kelly one. My life wasn't normal or stable so I would dream about a life like the ones in the movies. Usually you have these dreams of love when you are in your 20s but I was only 13 or 14. I picked up other girls and had sex with them. At that young age I hadn't experienced much love in my life.

I did it with any woman I could put my hands on. As a young man, I was good-looking and it was easy for me to pick up girls. I didn't ask any questions. I didn't want to know anything about their families. I just wanted to have sex. I wanted them to love me without me loving them in return. I didn't want to care about anybody but I felt I needed someone to care about me. It was as if I was trying to prove something by having sex with one girl after another.

I never even had to go to a prostitute. I was good-looking and the girls loved the way I dressed – with my leather jacket, jeans and boots. They knew I was tough and they felt protected. I could get anything or anyone I wanted. I would go to a party with one girl and then show up at the next party with a different one.

I was only interested in myself.

Being touched by a woman was something good, something new. But I didn't even get to know their names. It was like driving a car – it didn't mean anything.

Every time we moved, I met new girls. The Plateau Mont Royal was so large that even moving two or three streets over was like moving into a new neighborhood – with a different bunch of girls.

Every neighborhood also had its own gang. Unless you wanted to fight, you didn't go into another neighborhood.

But I was a loner – even as a young kid. I never wanted to be part of a gang. There was a club for training kids to become boxers. I didn't participate but I would wait outside the door for the guys to come out after practicing and say to them, "Hey, you are a boxer. Come with me."

I would beat them up.

Boxing has rules. In street fighting, there are no rules. In boxing, you use only your hands. In street fighting, you use your hands and your feet. I just wanted to hurt the guys. "I will kick you in the balls. I am going to kick you wherever. When you are done, I am going to kick you in the face."

I was passionate about hurting guys but I never hit a girl. Even if the girl had lied to me, I didn't do anything.

I was becoming a loner. Since I had developed a bad reputation in my neighborhood, we'd go to other neighborhoods to do bad stuff. We rode the trams, hanging onto the back.

I was about 17 in 1961 when I was arrested for attempted armed robbery, possession of a firearm, stolen car.

It was going to be simple. I had a partner who was going to be my driver. The plan was that I was to go inside the bank, jump over the counter and get the money and he would wait in the car to drive.

The robbery was successful. I was successful. But after getting in the car, the driver was so nervous – he was driving crazy. Suddenly the car was spinning around and round and round – we didn't have seat belts back then – and I was thrown out of the car onto the middle of the street.

I hit the dashboard so hard that I had injured my back so when I landed on my knees, I couldn't do anything else but crawl. So, I was crawling, and yelling at him. And he just started running away

I couldn't believe it. I yelled at him to stop and help me. But he didn't help me. He just left me there and took off.

I was writhing in pain. But the police didn't care. They handcuffed me and took me to the hospital in their car. You are always handcuffed – even if you are injured. Then I was taken to the police station where they took photographs, and fingerprints. They checked me over at the hospital and said I was OK. I just had water on the knee which I still have it to this day. I was cut up all over.

I wasn't scared. I didn't care about anything. At this point I hardly saw my family any more. Getting caught and being manhandled was part of the territory. I just didn't care.

I stayed in remand in the Bordeaux Prison, an old prison for men that still exists today – a holding place for guys who were sentenced to do provincial time. I stayed there while I was waiting for trial.

At the trial, I vividly remember the Judge, an elderly man with a distinctive white beard, who sentenced me to two years and I ended up in Saint Vincent de Paul Penitentiary.

CHAPTER FOUR
Zillion Cockroaches

There was the realization, "I am going to prison. This is me. My god, now I am in the real place. I am in prison."

Saint Vincent de Paul was one of the oldest prisons in Canada at that time. It was a dump. The layout was similar to Stony Mountain with the dome in the middle and the ranges radiating out from the center. When I walked into the prison I felt as if I was in a trance. As a kid, I had been violent. Now, I had walked into a jungle. Unconsciously, I probably said to myself, "If you don't learn to be the worst animal in the jungle, you are going to die. You are done. People will walk all over you."

I was sent to the youth wing. I was in the worst maximum a kid can be in his life.

You wouldn't believe how small my cell was. I could stand and touch both walls with my elbows. You had a little table that unfolded from the wall. You couldn't unfold your table and your bed at the same time. You had to unfold the bed, sit on the bed, and then unfold your table. There was no toilet and no water.

At night they gave you hot water in a bucket through the bars. They would come by and ask. "Do you want hot water?" Then you washed yourself with a cloth because you got a shower only once a week. Then the bucket became your toilet.

I still remember the first night as if it were yesterday. We got our meals in our cells. They passed a tray through the bars. I had just arrived that afternoon and I got a piece of cake. I said, "Oh my god! I am going to keep my piece of cake for later on tonight." I wrapped it up in a piece of toilet paper.

About 8:00 that night, I went to pick up my cake. There were a zillion cockroaches on it.

I discovered that when you turned on the lights, you could see them on your wall, on your ceiling, all over the place.

At first, I didn't know a soul in prison, so I just watched with horror. Later for fun we would bet on the cockroaches. If there were three cockroaches on the wall, you would choose one and the other guy would choose another. You bet a pack of tobacco. Which cockroach would reach the ceiling first? Gambling with cockroaches. It's a world I could never have imagined. When I was in my bed sleeping, I was afraid a cockroach would fall on me – on my chest. That first night in prison was incredible for me.

Then in the morning after you get out of your cell, you take the bucket in one hand and you get your tray, because you are going to go downstairs. They give you the bucket, they put some white lime in it and then you pick up your breakfast. You go back to your cell with your tray in one hand, and your empty bucket in the other – a simple in and out. It was just amazing.

Supper came on an all-metal tray which was good for smacking people's heads. We would get into arguments at night when the guy was making too much noise in his cell.

You say, "Shut up." He says, "No, you shut up." You wait and when he comes by you, you smack him with the tray.

You are crazy. I was crazy. The tin cups had handles and when you smacked the guy on the side of the head with your cup, he would go down. Everything was a tool for me in this jungle.

But I didn't panic. I knew that I would only be in prison for a while – only two years, and then I would be out. So, I cut myself off from everything. I did not even have a visitors list. I didn't want to see anybody. There were no visits. But having visitors was a privilege. If you didn't do your chores or if you acted out, your visits were cut off. I said, "Go ahead. Cut off my visits. I don't have visitors anyway. Stick it." I didn't want anything. I know my brother tried to visit me, but I turned him down. There was nothing that I wanted to have from anybody. I was an animal.

Nobody had a hold on me. You can't force someone to do anything if they just don't care. When you don't care if you live or die, when you have nothing in life to live for, you can't be manipulated. I got to a point – that I didn't care if I would be killed by someone stronger than me or someone with more guts than me, or crazier than me. It is the way I was. I felt it was the honorable way to live – or die – given the situation I was in.

Then six months later, I heard that my partner, the guy I trusted with my life, who had left me lying in the street, had been charged with something else and was now in the same penitentiary.

I was pissed.... I value loyalty. From the very beginning, when I had started doing small robberies, I expected people to do exactly what I told them to do. My word was law and if you breached that word, I would get the person back one day. He left me lying there in the street. I would have put my life on the line for him and I expected him to do the same for me. If something had happened to my partner in the bank, if someone had jumped him, I was prepared to shoot. I would do it instinctively. I had trained my mind.

I arranged with the guards to come into the yard and I gave it to him. I just beat the shit out of him. It was not enough to just punch and kick him. "I am so thrilled to see you, you son of a bitch. You should have never done that. You left me there as if I was dead. When I asked you to take me with you, you never did."

I was so full of anger and hate that I couldn't stop myself. I just gave it to him and gave it to him and beat him to a pulp. He ended up in the hospital.

He never went out in the population after that. Never.

But the guards – grabbed me and put me in the hole.

The hole in those days was different than it is now. That's where they put you when you breach the rules. You can get 15 days, 30 or 45 days in the hole. When you are sentenced to 30 days in the hole you are served eight slices of bread a day, and every seven days you get a meal.

Imagine – one meal every seven days! The rest of the time they give you only bread. The only thing you can keep in your cell is a towel. After taking your shower, you wrap your bread up in it and make a pillow out of it. You don't want to eat dry bread or even fresh bread without anything else. I just said, "Stick it. I don't care."

I was so disciplined and self-controlled. I never ate the bread. It was more useful as a pillow. They gave me a book – a Bible. I never opened a page. Never. I didn't want anything from anybody. I was so angry and filled with hatred. I hated the people of God.

CHAPTER FIVE
Hostage Taking.

After I got out, we started to rob big stores. I had a gun and my partner had a gun. We became quite ferocious. We were going after anyone.

We were also starting to look at kidnapping bank managers. In those days the bank manager had the combination for the vault.

We would kidnap both the bank manager and his wife at their home. If you did not take his wife as well, by the time you got the money, he would have called the cops.

Controlling the wife was important to us.

We would say to him, "You are going to go to the bank. You are going to get the money or she is dead. You have a choice." We would let him go and then contact him from a pay phone.

There were public phone booths all along the streets in Montreal in those days. "Come and meet us here with the money." We would release his wife when he gave us the money.

I think we planned three of these kidnappings and robberies the same year but we only did one and we didn't get arrested.

These kidnappings and robberies took a lot of planning. First, we would go to the bank and check out the bank manager's office. Once we knew who the manager was, we would wait and then try to follow him home. Sometimes it took seven tries before we discovered where he lived. You have to be patient. Sometimes you lose him in the traffic. Sometimes he isn't going home. Eventually you find out his address.

Once you know his address, you check out the neighborhood. You check out everything. You watch in the morning, all day and in the evening. Does he have a wife? Kids? Is there a second car parked at the house at night? If there is only one car, chances are it's just the bank manager and his wife living in the house.

The day of the robbery, you go early in the morning and ring the doorbell. When someone comes to the door, you say, "Sorry my car is stuck and I've been hurt. Can I come in and call the cops?" There were no cell phones back then. As soon as the door opened, we knew we were OK. But we wanted to get inside immediately, because if the screaming started right at the door, the neighbors might hear it.

As soon as we got through the door, we yelled, "Down! Not a word." My partner would go upstairs and get the bank manager's wife. Then we would go outside and get both of them in the car. We would take off and go to the bank. We don't go inside the bank with him. His wife is our guarantee that he will get the money for us. The bank manager's job is to go into the bank, wait until the time he can open the vault, open it and take the money. We tell him that someone is watching him. If he makes a move, his wife will be dead before he gets out of the bank. He is terrified.

The women always cried.

But we reassured them, "We don't want to hurt you. Your husband will do just as we asked him. Then you will be free to go. Don't worry." You might not be able to get the wife settled down. She might go nuts. You just have to keep saying, "Nothing is going to happen to you. It is just money. A man won't gamble his wife for money. You don't even own that money. It is owned by the bank." Just as we played with the bank manager's mind, we played with the wife's mind.

I was completely out of control pulling armed robberies – sometimes one a week, depending. If I had money in my pocket, I was okay. But when I ran out of money I would steal.

One plan we had – the one I was caught for – was never really successful. We had made tools to fish down into the outside bank deposits for their night deposit bags, but they caught us. I was arrested at an apartment for a series of armed robberies, possession of a gun, attempted robbery and possession of tools and a stolen car. I was 21 years old. Second time I was imprisoned.

May 10, 1964. The judge gave me 14 years and 10 months in the federal penitentiary.

Once again, I was in Saint Vincent de Paul Penitentiary – on the adult side now.

And then my girlfriend, who was in love with me, came to visit with her mother. I'd been arrested almost at the same time. We were having intercourse all the time. We went to the priest office, because it was a special visit. Her mother came with her. And it is where I found out she was pregnant.

When her mom told me I laughed at her. "Fuck you." They cut the visit right away, and they went out. I didn't care. Her mother was so angry, she said she wanted me to be killed. To me that was like saying "I want you to eat a chocolate bar." I didn't care. I have nothing to give, and I have nothing to take.

They charged me with statutory rape, having sex with a minor.

The fact that I have been having sex with the underage girl, but she was16, and I didn't know that at that time, I think it was14. But even if I had known, I don't think it would have made a difference.

Then her mother wanted a judge to hang me. She hated my guts, she hated me, she hated everything I represent.

Later I said to my girlfriend, "Listen, I like you but I am not in love with you. And I got 14 years and 10 months to serve. Why would you waste your life and time with a guy like me? I would like to see my son, but the best life for him would be with somebody else." And it is what she did.

She gave birth on January 3, 1965 to my son.

She married somebody else, she got two more children. I saw my son, he was about twelve, thirteen years old, and he lost an arm in the bike accident.

A car hit his bicycle and he had lost his arm. She used to send me pictures of him, I got some at home. She used to send me picture of him, a baby, two years old, five years old, but I was not attracted to her in any way. That is the right word. Physically I was attracted to her, she was a good-looking young girl, but I don't have love to give to anybody.

I don't think I would have been a good father.

Extreme violence was the norm for a maximum penitentiary. The most violent guys in Montreal were in there and I wanted to be the worst of the worst. When I beat up that guy in the yard and they had to fire, they knew that there was real danger. More people could jump in and get involved. I was always protecting myself. There were some predators in there and I knew what they were doing.

At that time the prison had four floors of cells. You were in your cell night and day. You worked for two hours, went to your cell, then you picked up your meal and ate it in your cell. You did everything in your cell. The blocks had toilets and sinks.

In the 60s, the mentality in the penitentiary was kill to survive or be killed. I was always considering the possibility: survive or die? I would always go the extra mile when the other guys would not. For me it was, "Hey, let's go man. Let's go. Yah, you better kill me because I am coming to kill you." Here I am – 21 years old in prison for the second time. I had already made a name for myself. A guy who is in for two years hears this and thinks, "Don't fuck around with Rene because he is nuts."

We played tennis or racquetball, football in the snow or on the gravel with no equipment. I was the craziest football player they could ever have. I was not playing hockey to play hockey but to hurt others. I hit someone so hard that I shattered a bone in my shoulder and I still have pain there, when I raise my arm.

There was only one inmate in each cell. I started to show people that no one is going to fuck around with Rene. I started to fight. I was good at it. People told me I was crazy to take on the guys that I took on. But I never backed down. I said, "You are going to have to kill me."

Once someone starts fighting with you, they know that they will have to kill you in order to stop you. It really isn't a fair fight, because I didn't care. When you have nothing in life, when you don't want to love anybody, when you cannot love anybody, you don't have anything to lose. You have only hatred and anger. When you have nothing in life, you don't want anything.

I didn't want any visits – absolutely none. I was afraid if they started to give me visits, they would want something in return. One day I fucked with a guy. We were playing racquetball. I walked behind him, touched his racquet and he started to scream. I took his racquet from him, and I just started punching him. They had to fire a rifle to stop me from beating him up. They were screaming, "Stop! We are going to shoot." I knew that, but I didn't care. I just wanted him. The rest didn't matter. I didn't care about what happened to me. It was deliverance for me. It's the way I look at life. It is deliverance if someone shoots you. Who cares? Kill me if you want. I don't care.

I admit - I was suicidal, self-destructive. Because of everything that happened to me as a kid, I became a self-destructive adult every day of my life. I wanted to die. I wanted to disappear. I didn't want to feel anything. My stomach was tense. I was like a time bomb. I don't know how I managed to live like this for so long. But you become used to it – it becomes you. When you are in the jungle, only the strongest animal survives. The rest die. That is what I projected. I became the strongest animal anyone would ever see in that jail and they called me the crazy one.

It is funny. I always enjoyed playing the part. I enjoyed being strong enough to beat the shit out of anyone. I enjoyed the part where they shoot me and then kill me. Nobody cared. When you have nothing in life, you don't want anything. I know I was an animal. It was impossible to control an animal like me.

We knew there was a guy upstairs who was a skinner – a guy who raped a girl – a sexual predator. Skinners were my favorite target. We were screaming at him, "Hang yourself, you peace of shit. Tomorrow we are going to kill you." All night we yelled at him, "Hang yourself."

He did hang himself. We wanted that. When morning came and I knew that they had cut him down, it was triumph for me. The guys were scared, and they didn't want to do anything. Never, never.

I felt that I had done justice. I felt that my kind of crime was different than the crimes of the skinners. All the inmates like me wanted the skinners to die, to hang themselves. We whispered continuously, "Hang yourself, you piece of shit." We called them everything in the book. Then they would hang themselves. They put the skinners away. It always took a week or two before they could put them away. During that time they were left in their cells and we wanted to throw gas and a lighter on them so that they would burn.

I had made my name, my reputation. The English speakers called me "Crazy"— the French speakers, "Pit bull." Those are the best names I could have been given. I was happy. I was a somebody. They knew who I was. You make a name for yourself by what you are doing in life. Some people make a name for themselves as doctors. I made a name for myself as a criminal – a criminal who would never give up. I was a "sick puppy" and that is when they put me in the psychiatric wing.

I know. I was declared a psychopath in the penitentiary. Maybe I was. Maybe I was not. I don't know, because I didn't even know the meaning of the word psychopath. I graduated from Grade Seven. Although I attended Grade Nine for a while, I quit school after that and never went back. My education was quite limited. Even when I was in school, I didn't study at all. So, I didn't know what that meant.

They gave me medication. Because they think you are crazy, they never open your cell door, unless you are going to see a doctor. They wanted to calm me with "bug juice" – medication dissolved in water – but I threw it against the wall. I always said, "What the fuck do you want, you fuckin'… Fuck you. I am not crazy. You are crazy." I was just angry. "You are fuckin' crazy. Leave me the fuck alone. Leave me in my cell. I don't care if I ever get out." I didn't care. You get to the point where you become comfortable in your cell. You never have to do anything.

I tried to prove to them that I was a real psychopath. Everything I did was to show I was more violent than anyone else. No one was violent towards me. It was the kind of jungle I had lived in since I was five years old. I protected myself by being violent towards others. I made my point. They knew that if they came at me, I would fuckin' kill them. I felt safe and I slept at night.

You can train your mind to do anything you want. You can set your mind to destroy the world, if you want. I know that because I did it so often. The mind is the strongest part of any human being on the planet. When we lose our mind, we don't have anything. We are finished. We are done. I intentionally developed my mind to become stronger every day by using hatred and anger and destruction.

This was the best way for me. Don't ask for anything. Refuse anything they want to give you. As a result, nobody can manipulate you. No one can do anything to get you.

In 1965, they put me in the psychiatric wing. They thought that I was crazy.

I was so violent that they locked me up in a cell for 23 ½ hours out of every day for six months. They were not able to control me with the punishment they had there.

Two guards would come to the door. I would put my hands through the hole in the door and they would cuff me. Then they would open the door and walk me towards the yard where they would take off the handcuffs. The yard was so small you could only walk in circles. It wasn't too bad in the summer but it was very cold in winter. We got one shower a week in the penitentiary. You took your shower really fast. It was cold because the shower was in the same place where we changed for hockey. The door was always open so you took your shower, ran out, got dressed and went back to your cell to get warm.

I was a wild animal. Sometimes to get my hatred out, I was hitting the wall until my hands were bloody.

I'm not a big guy – five foot eight and a half, 160 pounds. My god, I fought with some of the biggest guys you can see in prison – guys who were doing weights all the time. Although I'm not big, I can hit with both hands like a hammer. And I am a righty, and my left is the worst to take a guy down. I wanted to be the king of this jail. I fought a big guy in the yard. The guard had to shoot to stop me from totally beating up the guy.

Even at that time, my only goal was to become a better and smarter criminal. The bigger criminals were the guys I looked up to. I never fought with them. I admired the guys who robbed trains and got four or five million dollars.

I never used drugs. I had smoked pot in the inmate center but, apart from that, I was not into drugs. I never drank in my life. Some people get into a criminal lifestyle because they are alcoholics or drug addicts but I never did drugs or alcohol. So how do you explain how I got to this place? I was on a path of self-destruction. I was damaged from way back and I kept damaging myself. Something was wrong in my brain. I didn't care about my life or anyone else's.

Things always took place in the yard. You start with the guy. You say, "Hey. I am Rene." The guy replies, "We know who you are." They liked me because they knew I would never back down. You judge a person by their actions. If you are afraid that someone wouldn't cover your back in a bank, you don't want that person around you. But when you see a guy who is crazy like me, they know that they just need to teach him the proper way and he will be OK. I learned many things from these guys -- how to manage your gun, how to cover your partner. When you walk into a bank you don't shoot at the people. You shoot at the ceiling.

The most dangerous guy I ever met in prison was French – about my size and wore glasses.

I was attracted to guys like him. They were my heroes, my teachers. I felt that I had everything except the knowledge and experience of how to rob a bank in the proper way. It's easy to go into a bank but if you don't have a getaway plan, all you'll get is your name in the paper for attempted robbery and you'll be arrested. The key element for any job is the getaway. Don't even try to steal ten million dollars without a getaway plan because you'll never get the ten million. That's what they taught me. I owe everything to these guys. I became really smart after that. I just kept on learning.

Then some guy said, "Rene, cool off a little bit. We would like to get you as a partner. Try to get the hell out of here. You will never get out the way you are going. You are going to serve the full 14 years."

Then I started to be a bit better. When I cooled down, they thought I was an angel, because I was the worst devil they had in that prison when I first came in.

CHAPTER SIX
Shoot Out

I had been released from prison only three months prior and I was already planning my next bank robbery. This time it was a bank in Rosemont – the biggest. There were four of us involved – three of us to rob the bank. David and Gaetan were my partners with one driver of the getaway car. His name was Leonard.

I'll never forget the day. I had planned the moment for months. It had to be the right bank, right partners, right time of the day. And it was.

We parked on the street in front of the bank. We pulled nylon stockings over our faces as masks, and ran in.

I was the last one to leave the car, following my partners with the machine gun in my hands, covering them so that they would be safe.

Once inside the bank, I started barking orders, "Everybody on the ground. Don't move or I will kill you."

I fired a round of bullets into the ceiling with my M1 rifle they used in Vietnam. I also had a spare gun, a Mark III Commando with a double clip strapped to my waist. I walked the floor yelling and swearing at the people to lie down and not move, threatening that if they didn't, they were all going to die. And I meant it – and they knew it.

We had to control the scene. It was the only way we could get the money. We treated it like a job.

Because I was the one with the machine gun, I was the boss.

As the boss, I am the one who is looking around – covering the other two as they went about their business. We have only seconds to do our work. I'm the one who keeps my eye on the time. When I say it's time, they have to stop, so I'm the one who is tasked with keeping my eye on the time. When I say it's time, they have to stop whatever they are doing. When I say go, we go.

My two partners were jumping over the counters and scooping up the money from the tills. In no time their bags were full. Money was spilling....

They were fast.

When they had emptied as many tills as I thought reasonable, I called to them that their time was up! They stopped everything, and we raced out of the building, leaving the people still screaming and lying on the floor.

Our driver was ready for us. The doors were already open, and all the windows were rolled down.

Every time you rob a bank you never keep the windows closed, because if someone shoots towards the windows, the glass shards could come inside the car and hit you in the face, a shotgun effect.

Because I was covering my partners with the gun, I was the last one to reach the car.

Even though the back door was ajar, it was not open enough for me to get in so I fumbled with it. Our driver was anxious and was already gunning the motor. I had to do a running jump into that moving car – just barely making it. Our hearts were racing. There hadn't been a moment to spare. We had done it in the allotted time –two minutes – and we had to get out of there – fast.

We were going to be millionaires!

Already we were feeling that relief of a job done. We were safe. We were about to celebrate, when a huge bulletproof City of Montreal truck pulled up in front of us – blocking us.

Police!

Using a bullhorn, the cops were ordering us, "Surrender! We have you surrounded!"

I yelled at Leonard, our driver, "Fuck them. We are not surrendering."

I pulled out my pistol and put it to his head, "If you don't go, I am going to kill you."

He drove like a maniac, and managed to get around the truck.

But by then the bullets were beginning to fly, so I started shooting back. I started acting like a wild man. I still don't know what came over me. I was just shooting at anything and everything because I didn't know where the bullets were coming from....

My partner, David, who was sitting right in front of me, got hit – a bullet right in his head. As if in slow motion, I saw David just slip down in his seat.

My other partner, Gaetan, who was sitting with me in the back of the car, was also shooting from his side of the car and got hit by two bullets that came from the trunk and hit him in the back.

But nothing was going to stop me. I kept yelling at the driver, "You have to keep going or I'll kill you." But eventually, the car came to a stop. He was slumped over the wheel. The cops had used a shotgun – and there were two or three pellets that had been shot through the windshield into his face.

So I was the only one left able to move. I picked up my automatic M1 because my Mark III was empty by then, jumped out of the car and started to run, and run, and shoot. I would have killed anyone in my way. I didn't care that there were people on the street – screaming. I didn't care. I was a maniac. I just wanted to get away. They were right after me.

I have to say the cops were motivated. We had robbed a few banks before, and they knew by our style that this was a repeat job. They were frustrated that they hadn't been able to capture us, so they wanted us stopped even if it meant killing us on the job.

In turn, we were becoming more savage. Because we knew the cops wanted to kill us, we thought, "If we are going to die, they are going to die before we do." We didn't care, and I was the worst one because of my hatred towards anyone with any kind of authority.

Finally, the cops surrounded me by a school wall. I turned my machine gun on myself and I tried to kill myself. Right on the spot. I thought to myself, "If I am going back to jail, I am going to die." But the gun jammed.

They jumped on me, and they took me down.

They put the handcuffs on me, and took me to the Parthenais Jail. It was a brand-new jail at the time. All I could think of was my partners.

As it turned out, the driver, who got shotgun pellets in his face, was OK. They took Gaetan to the hospital and he was OK. David was killed.

I just didn't understand it. "How the hell was it not me? How the hell was I not hit?" All the bullets came right through the vehicle. "Why?"

That question: "Why had the bullets bypassed me?" drove me wild. I blamed the cops. You always blame the shooter. Later when they counted the holes in the car, there were 72. I don't know how many bullets passed straight through – we'll never know – but they counted 72 bullet holes in the car.

It took me a while to process this. First of all, I had to figure out how the police knew about us.

No one knew. We would spend the night before we did the robbery in my apartment, together – with no booze. We had to be sober. It is what we did whenever we did a robbery – spend the night together.

But I sensed that something was happening that night, there was something not quite right – especially with David.

I liked David. We were not extremely close but he was a good partner. At the time he was going out with my girlfriend's sister. He beat her up often. I was aware that he beat her up because when you are someone's partner, you also end up as a partner with his girlfriend or his wife. I didn't like to see his abusive nature, because I was raised as a kid to never touch a woman, never beat up a woman, never raise a hand to a woman. I knew he was beating her up but I did not know how bad it had gotten.

But the night prior to our being together, David beat the crap out of her – Micheline his girlfriend. He really beat her up badly – most of the time alcohol was involved. Then after, he would be sorry and he would cry and she would cry. He would say, "I didn't mean to…." It was the typical family violence. This time, trying to make her feel better, he promised her, "Tomorrow I am going to take you somewhere special. I'm going to have money. We are going to be rich. We are going to build a new house…. We are going to do another robbery."

Micheline's mother was in the kitchen and she heard David tell Micheline that we were going to do the bank in Rosemont. But when David came to the apartment to spend the night with us, he didn't tell me what had happened. It's the first rule of robbing banks. You're not supposed to talk to anyone about your plans to rob a bank, so you don't tell your partners that you have just beaten up your girlfriend… and that you might have talked too much.

Upset at David, the mother tipped off the police.

The next morning, we started off for the bank – completely oblivious of any of this… and it was David that paid for it.

They sent me to Parthenais, a brand-new building, a remand center, where guys were kept prior to their trial.

They took me and locked me up in a cell on the tenth floor. The eleventh floor was the roof with bars – where you went to take a walk during the day. Nobody wanted to go up there, because it was cold like hell.

All I could think of was that David had died. I wasn't able to eat for about seven days. I was just sick inside. I felt so bad. All I could think of was trying to escape.

Actually, we tried to escape – but the attempt failed. I was at the end of my rope by then.

Back then you were allowed to smoke in your cells. I smoked at the time and asked for my cigarettes and matches. The guards would come by with the matches to light your cigarette. They were supposed to light your cigarette through the door – but my guard was new and gave me the package, smokes and matches.

That's when I decided that I was done. I was desperate and depressed. I just wanted to die. It was finished.

I used the matches to ignite the straw-filled mattress. I couldn't believe how quickly it caught fire. I also didn't realize that they had covered the walls with a flammable metallic paint.

When the mattress lit up, the flames leaped, and suddenly all the walls turned into fire. I sat in the middle of my cell that had turned into an inferno, and I didn't know what to do.

Oh my god! The fire swirled around and around the walls. It was incredible how that paint burned. I was sitting helpless in the middle of the cell, and I felt like bacon sizzling in the pan. I was burning all over – on my back, on my arms. I was screaming.

The place was instantly filled with smoke – alerting everyone to the fire. The fire alarms were ringing.

I will never forget the name of the person who rescued me – Jacques. He was a social worker for the guys at the inmate center.

He was right outside my door. He didn't have keys so he screamed at the guards. "Open the door! If you don't let him out of his cell, I will testify against you in court if he dies. I guess they could have left me in there to die.

But they listened, and at that point they opened my cell door. I got up – out – and then fell outside the door. They said, "Don't touch him." I just lay there writhing in pain.

They saw my skin was all gone, and they knew the pain must be excruciating. When you cook bacon and the grease goes on your hand, it is painful. That's what I felt all over my back and all over my body. The pain was unbelievable.

When the police came, they didn't take me to the hospital in an ambulance but put me in the back seat of the car, covered with a sort of tinfoil blanket – something that couldn't stick to my skin. I ended up at Saint Luc Hospital.

At the hospital, they put me under. I'm not sure what happened after that because I was totally out of it. I was in a coma for seven days. They didn't know if I would survive or not.

Obviously, I did survive.

When I woke up, I felt that I had failed again. I had really wanted to die. I didn't really care how. At the time I thought the only way was to set the cell on fire. But I learned that burning alive was a terrible way to die. I was under medical treatment for three months and then they shipped me to Bordeaux Jail in Montreal.

From time to time they would take me to the hospital to have skin grafts done. It's amazing what they did and how I look now. You have three layers of skin. They cut through just one layer of skin with a knife, as if they are cutting cheese. Then they roll and roll. They took skin from both my thighs and grafted it onto my upper arm.

CHAPTER SEVEN
Attempted Escapes

I tried my first escape when they sent me to Parthenais Jail. It was a brand-new building, a remand center, where guys were kept prior to their trial.

I was still upset about the death of David, and I told my partner, "I am not staying here. I am going to die or I will escape."

We were locked up on the tenth floor, but I didn't care. I don't like heights, but I knew that it was face my fear or die.

On every floor of the prison, there was a fire hose, because if a guy or the cell started to burn, they needed to extinguish it. I don't know how long the hose was. I had a plan to escape from there, by cutting the bars, getting through the window, taking the fire hose and sheets to go down the ten floors.

I talked to my girlfriend, and my partner talked to his girlfriend. They were sisters, and they agreed to help us. I asked my girlfriend to buy me a pair of shoes. "Cut the front or the back and put two metal sawblades inside." Our girlfriends smuggled the blades in and we cut through the bars. They didn't have metal detectors back then. We would take the blades and start cutting through the bars on the window.

Between the two of us we had four blades inside the prison. There were three bars that we had to cut through before we could open the window.

I knew it was risky. I knew we could die, but my mind was strictly set on dying. I didn't want to do another 20 years. I had done enough already. We went for broke.

There was a fire hose that could go down 50 or 60 feet but that wasn't far enough. Since the bed sheets were changed every week, we kept a sheet each week and put it on our bed, to look as if the bed was made. The intention was to tie the extra sheets to the hose to make up the difference.

We cut and we cut. We always found a time to cut away at the bars.

Finally, we had cut through the three bars. We said, "OK. Tomorrow is the day. We are going." I asked my girlfriend and his girlfriend to get us a van and two shotguns and maybe a couple of handguns. I told them to park the car under our window, leave the guns in - leave the key and we would see them later that night.

We tied all the sheets together and the hose was ready. I took the hose and started going out of the window.

I thought we had everything covered. The staff would walk around and check on everything and then they would go back and sit down for a few hours. I thought we had timed them and planned this well.

We had a van parked below the tenth floor, with the shotgun and handguns. We were ready for war, if it came to that. When you are desperate and ready to die, you can become the most dangerous human being on the planet, because you don't care if you die.

But the guards came in and jumped on me, right when I was going through the window. They caught me right in the window sill.

They locked me up in the cell.

The second escape was from another prison – Archambault. This time I was smarter about it. Through wheeling and dealing – I was promoted to the kitchen. I served meals to the staff at lunch. When I worked there, I always wore a nice shirt and a clean pair of pants.

Sometimes I asked the staff for a key so that I could clean on both sides of the door. The staff walked in and out. Sometimes they came from outside for lunch.

There was the kitchen, the staff lunch room, and that led to the administration building which – of course -- led to the outside. What they didn't realize was that the same key fit the door at the other end that led right outside. All I had to do was unlock the door and I could escape.

I got my partner hired so he could come work with me in the staff mess. I was good with food and the staff trusted me. When you want someone to trust you, often it is going to appeal to the stomach through the food you provide them. Especially in prison, they like you to cook for them when they see that you don't put anything in their food. Sometimes inmate cooks would contaminate the staff food with pee and spit. I never did.

In this job we wore beige pants and golf shirts. I had the key and the plan. We were going to walk out on Sunday afternoon because lots of people were visiting.

If someone saw us walking out, they would think that we were staff.

The only thing I would have to do is wait there for that perfect moment.

It was Saturday night; we were in the prison lounge playing cards. We were all ready to go the next day.

Then Coco, the head of the Devil's Disciples later known as the Hells Angels - a rapist - came at me and said, "I want to fight you, you son of a bitch." I never liked him, and I had never had anything to do with him. I never talked to him. He was about my size. Yet, he came at me. "I am fuckin' going to beat the shit out of you." Then he punched me.

I thought to myself, "Don't fuckin' do that. I have something planned for tomorrow." I looked over at my partner and said, "Gaetan, what the fuck am I going to do?"

He said, "Do it!"

The first shot I gave Coco, he went right through a table. I was so angry that he was making me miss my escape. I hit him hard and tried to kill him with one punch. The guys watching were very happy.

I said, "I don't want to fight you Coco."

Then he gave me another shot.

My partner said, "Give it to him, Rene."

The guards came out through the little door with their guns and said, "Stop."

All the inmates got up and went to the door so that the guard wasn't able to shoot. The inmates used their bodies as a shield so that the guards couldn't stop the fight. They really wanted this biker to get it.

Did I ever give it to him! I broke his jaw and his eye socket. The bone from his eye socket went a quarter of an inch from his temple. He was in such bad shape that every time I punched him, he was bouncing over the table. I broke his thighs.

I was out of my mind. It was not me who was fighting but the devil. That is how he saw me – how they all saw me – as the devil. I just wanted to take him down any way that I could. I don't how many times he went down. I always let him get up, and I hit him again and again until he passed out on the side of the table. I completely beat the shit out of him.

The guys were all standing at the door, so that the guard couldn't shoot to stop the fight. I stopped hitting him only when he wasn't moving anymore.

He ended up in the hospital. For a guy to get beaten up and go to a hospital outside the penitentiary, you have to be pretty bad. They said I could have killed him because his bone was almost through his temple. I broke all the eye sockets. I really gave it to him.

After the fight finished, I went to see his big bodyguard. I said, "Get up. It's your turn." I bent over him, "Listen, you piece of shit. Why don't you get up? I am in good shape tonight for another one."

He never moved from his chair.

They locked me up in the hole. He went to the Queen Mary Hospital in Montreal. They didn't let me out of the hole until he was out of danger. When they saw that he was OK, that he wasn't going to die, they let me out of the hole.

Everybody in the jail was happy that I had beat him up, because those two were the worst scum of the prison. Bikers tried to do in jail what they did on the street. They were never able to do anything to me because I did nothing to them. When they want to get rid of a guy, they befriend him and then they get him hooked on drugs, and the first thing you know, you got the pill, you take it and then you are dead.

But they didn't know how to get rid of me. So, they sent their tough man to get me. When they saw what I did to that tough man, they backed off.

After that his bodyguard tried to become my friend, but I knew he was just scum. He wanted me to take drugs from him, and I would have died. There is no doubt.

It was my life. I was always ready to rumble. During all the years I spent in jail, I never wore slippers or pajamas. I was always ready – fully dressed in my boots, jeans and T-shirt until they locked me up in my cell at night. It was never easy to sit down and watch TV with me. I didn't nap much. I was always ready for action.

It is funny in prison how things happen. I was not the most liked person but between him and me, they hated him more than me.

The third escape attempt I made grenades in prison.

There were about ten inmates involved with this escape attempt. The organization was incredible! Each of us had a job. The food was prepared by the inmates in the minimum and loaded into trucks to be delivered to the maximum. The cook – the guy who worked in the kitchen -- knew exactly which cart would be delivered to our range – so he made sure that the powder, as well as a gun and six sticks of dynamite that had been secured by his friend on the outside, were on that specific cart – hidden in the food.

At supper time, everything was carefully timed. There was a cart for every range. They would drive to the penitentiary and go through the special entrance. There were three units in that penitentiary on two storeys. There was one truck per unit and each truck had 16 to 18 carts. Since everybody was in a hurry, they didn't bother doing searches.

My job was making grenades. You had to be resourceful getting supplies. Guys would get me little jars, like baby food jars, from the crafts area. Another guy who worked in the kitchen in minimum had a friend on the street who got the powder for the grenades.

I worked on the grenades strictly from eleven o'clock to midnight. Not before, because after every inmate was locked up, you could hear a pin drop in the prison. Every time a door was opened, you knew the guards were doing their rounds -- so you put everything aside and pretended you were asleep. As soon as they were finished, I would start back to work.

It was also dangerous. In those days, I smoked three packs of cigarettes a day. One night, as I lit up a cigarette, I said to myself, " What am I doing here making grenades? I am going to blow myself up!" I stopped smoking the same day. I never touched a cigarette again. It was a life and death situation.

It was my job to hide all the supplies for the grenades in my cell – jars, nuts and bolts, wicks and powder as well as the gun and dynamite. I couldn't make the grenades in one night. It took about three nights to make one grenade. The only place for me to hide the supplies was in the heating system. There was an eight-or-nine-inch square vent in the floor where the hot air came through. I broke the cement all around it and shoved my supplies into the duct.

I used a coat hanger to push the stuff in. It was flexible so that I could also retrieve my things. I put the gun in first, then the dynamite and then the grenades in last. I worked every night and this was the only way I could hide everything securely.

I put caulking around the opening and then I painted the floor with paint I had taken from the shop. It was a masterpiece every night.

Then there was this inmate, Gilles. I have never met anyone so technical who was able to use his hands that way. Gilles slept on the first floor, in the same unit as me, but on a different range. In this escape plan, his job was to go down to the basement and dig through the wall. He managed to make some kind of a tool for digging. I never saw it.

The only time he could work on this was between 5:30 and 6:30 p.m. -- shower time.

It was the same for every inmate. There were two showers at the end of the range. Three inmates would have their showers at the same time every night.

Gilles never took a shower but used this time to dig. After showers, they opened all the ranges in the prison. People can go out into the yard or watch TV in a little room around the tower. There is free movement for about ten minutes.

He always stayed in his cell to dig. He dug through the floor under his bed and then through the walls to go under the Administration Building.

There were seven guys on his range that were part of it and they always covered up for him.

It took the guy a long time to dig through the walls - for 3 months. I believe that he probably broke through ten walls until he was under the administration area. We were waiting....

My grenades were finished and I was waiting for the guy downstairs to tell me, "Rene, bring the stuff downstairs. We'll be ready in two days. He is almost done. He is under the administration."

Today when I think about this, I am glad we did not get through. But at that time, my hatred was increasing every day. What would I have done when I got out?

I didn't care if I had gotten killed. Any one of us could have been killed.

You throw a grenade.

You throw dynamite.

You start to shoot.

One guy had a gun – not me. I would have had two grenades and a stick of dynamite. The other guys might have had two grenades or one grenade and dynamite.

If there were shots, we might have been able to defend ourselves a little but we know that someone would have died. I thrived on that.

My mind was so defective that excitement for me meant being part of the action and getting even with those who had put me in jail. I had, in fact, put myself in jail.

But, at that time, I always put the blame on everybody else. "That son of a bitch. If he hadn't come into the bank, I wouldn't have been arrested."

I always deflected any responsibility. It was mind boggling. I was so anxious.

He had just one wall to go through to get to the tower. Our escape plan was to walk to the tower, get the guard there and then just take off. It was a desperate plan and we were ready to do anything. I was the guy to throw the grenade.

The night of the planned escape, a keeper – supervisor – whose office was beside the administration went into the administration building to take a leak.

He heard noises. Then he remembered that no one was working. So why was he hearing that noise? Specifically, why was he hearing noises from below the main floor? Tap. Tap. Tap. The sounds got loud and louder. So the keeper went down to investigate and he saw my friend.

Gilles started to run and go back to his cell on his floor, but they came down and they saw the dynamite, the grenades and the gun. They grabbed him right away, and they came and grabbed about ten of us. They shut down the prison.

They took the ten of us and moved us all to different cells.

It was only then I realized that in my three main attempts to escape prison that in each one – just as the plan was to be executed – something intervened at the very last moment. Days, even months of scheming and planning -- all for naught.

It was almost as if there was a destiny – a plan for my life to keep me alive.

CHAPTER EIGHT
Visiting Room

I did more shit – so they shipped me to Stony Mountain Penitentiary. It took almost the whole day to travel. It was a nice November day – not stormy and not cold.

It was just a normal day – except that I was in shackles, not able to move, on the plane for the whole day.

On the plane, if someone was staring at me, I stared back at them. They were more afraid of me than I was of them.

After we arrived at the airport, an escort drove me right to Stony Mountain. They put me in the back for the night and, the next day, they put me on the range. I don't remember which unit I ended up in.

Stony Mountain was a medium security penitentiary built in 1874 – one of the worst prisons in Canada.

It was an old prison. Saint Vincent de Paul, Dorchester, Prince Albert, Kingston, and Stony Mountain. They were all pretty much the same. I was home.

The next morning, after I was put into population, I went to see my partner, Gaetan on another range. I started to chat with him about how things were in there. He told me that it was a shithole. "Hey, welcome to the real world."

So many guys knew me and my reputation. "Don't fuck around with Rene." I was home. I wanted to get out, but I was taking the wrong path to get out. I didn't want to be held accountable for parole. I didn't want to be held accountable for anything.

I still had attitude – but it was starting to change.

I was there for two years – when my life took a turn.

I was 36 years old – not a bad looking man – with hair down to my neck. Long hair was cool back then. I was in prison, Stony Mountain Institution, when my partner said, "Rene, I am having a visitor." I was immediately interested.

"You lucky bastard," I told him. "I don't think I have ever had a visit – not from family or anyone. Who is visiting you?"

He told me that he had, through an elderly nun volunteering in the chapel at Stony for years and years, met someone. That nun was the best old lady I have ever met in my life.

That is where my partner met his girlfriend. He said, "I am going to ask her to ask her sister if she wants to have a visit with you."

I said, "Do that. I want to see a woman, man."

He asked her, and she said OK.

She came to visit me two weeks later in Stony Mountain, after the paperwork was done. It had been about nine years since I had seen a woman close up and now I had one sitting right next to me. She was a good-looking woman, about 29 at that time.

"Oh my god, it is true."

The visiting room is kind of funny, because you walk out and then there is a corner – a cage where the staff are.

I'll never forget that first meeting.

At the end of the evening, she was leaning her head against the wall, right by the window. I kissed her on the cheek.

That was the first time I kissed Suzanne – Suzanne Tessier.

She left but that night she called her sister, and said, "I had to leave but he wants to see me again."

My partner came and told me that. I said to him, "Yes. Tell her to come back. I would be happy to see her."

I fell for her back then, and she fell for me. On the second visit I started kissing her and she let me kiss her. I started touching her but she didn't want me to touch her. She was not the kind of person who comes to visit to meet a guy.

She had broken up with her partner of ten years about a year before. She was on her own, by herself, and she didn't expect that any more than I. We both fell for each other, and she kept visiting me.

She blushed when I said to her, "That night when you had your head against the wall, I knew you wanted to see me again."

Suzanne kept visiting me.

I started to train in Stony Mountain. There was no program. I did it on my own. I was training to run the marathon in 1981, the second Manitoba Marathon. I started running the stairs. We had four sets of stairs. I would run up one set and come down the other – sometimes for two or three hours every day. I was just training – to be able to run a marathon. I didn't know if I could even run in the marathon.

Everyone started talking about what I was doing. For a change, they were saying things like, "This guy is not like the one we have on the file. In the 70s he was in Dorchester and all those other penitentiaries." I started talking with my parole officer in a good way. Before that it was, "Fuck you," and I only talked with people if I wanted to.

I just wanted to get out, but I wanted to get out the proper way. My motivation was to get out and be with Suzanne.

They agreed to let me go to the Rockwood Institution – a minimum security place. I had been a good meat cutter in Dorchester and Springhill and I became the meat cutter right away in Stony Mountain. They approved my move from Stony to Rockwood.

I started to train at Rockwood and asked for permission to go out at four in the morning to run around the house. They agreed and I was released to run for three hours. In those days there was no house. It was just a big building with a dormitory upstairs. Downstairs there was a kitchen and administration office. I always slept upstairs like everybody else and I went out to run in the mornings.

We weren't doing trailer visits – not yet – but we were preparing for that. I was trying to see if I could get a Temporary Absence (TA) to go to the marathon, because it was in Winnipeg. I didn't know what to do. If I raised the money for marathon, that would be something good I could do for the community. It would also help me but that wasn't my main goal.

My main goal was to get Suzanne. She was the one collecting the money for the marathon from family and friends. It wasn't a big chunk of money but she raised about $300 or $400.

When I asked for the first trailer visit, they agreed. It was everything I had hoped for. We grew close. I knew she was in love, and I was too. I had loved a woman before, but it was not the same thing. The woman before was like my partner in crime, because I got her to bring me the saw and everything I needed when I wanted to escape from the inmate centre. With Suzanne, it was different. She was innocent. She didn't have a clue what a guy from prison was like.

Suzanne was working for a company called Kimberly Clark.

She had worked there for years and had a good life.

She was renting a little house on Hindley Street that I called "Little house on the Hindley" instead of "Little house on the Prairie." It was a tiny house, but it was good for her, because she was on her own. There was only one bedroom. When her brother moved in with her for a while, he slept on the couch. Her sister moved in with her after that. When I asked for a TA (temporary absence) to go her place, they agreed.

I have forgotten the name of the guy who escorted me but I worked with him years later at Stony. I always had a good relationship with him. He was my Correctional Officer (CO2). Finally, I asked the warden if I could run the marathon. He said, "Yes, Rene, because I don't think that you are going to run away. You are going to run a real marathon."

And about two weeks later, I hurt a ligament in my leg but I kept on doing light training. I usually ran 10 or 15 miles a day but I couldn't do more than a mile a day with my injury. When you are training for a marathon, you need to run 10 or 15 miles to make sure you can do 26 miles. Twenty-six miles is the hardest thing to do, because you hit the wall after the 20th mile. I didn't know that then. I was in unbelievably good shape. Even when I came to Stony, I was doing push-ups and jogging in my cell. I just wanted to train and be in the best shape possible.

We went to Winnipeg for the marathon. There was an escort. What could he do but stay with Suzanne. They followed along, from place to place, to watch me running. I completed the whole marathon – all 26 miles – but after the 12th mile, I was able to use only one leg.

My other leg gave out but I did not stop – I finished the whole thing. Twenty-six miles – 42 kilometers. I did it in four hours and a bit, but for me the time was not important. I probably wouldn't have run it in much less than four hours, even with two good legs. I was not a fast marathon runner but a fast 100-yard runner. I humped it all the way after the 12th mile and finished. I couldn't give up. I couldn't stop.

My pride was everything. I had put everything I had into it. I just wanted to run. I didn't want them to see me stop and give up. My attitude was, "I am going to get that thing done and that's it." And I achieved that – I did it. They don't care how much time you take. You finish your marathon. You get the same thing as everybody else, and go back to the prison.

The next step was to ask for parole. I had received escorted TAs. I think I had had one or two unescorted TAs, when Suzanne came to pick me up with her car. At that time I was working for an Englishman who had been a baker at Buckingham Palace when he was 16. He taught me about being a baker.

This guy screamed at everybody – all the time – but he never screamed at me. I don't know why – I never asked him. I was just happy that he didn't scream at me. I didn't want to react to him. He always respected me. I think that he was trying to teach me something. He didn't have the patience to teach you, if you didn't want to learn – and I really wanted to be a baker. I wanted to know all about baking. He taught me how to make French pastry, and I can still do it. Then I asked for parole. The Parole Board approved me, but they didn't want me to live in Quebec or Manitoba.

Suzanne said her cousin lived in Nelson B.C. and asked if they would support Rene if we moved there. They wrote a letter of support to the parole board when I made parole on December 16, 1981. Pete and Andrée Maynard – thank you.

CHAPTER NINE
Surrounded by Mountains

The moment came – unbelievable. I walked out of the prison doors… on parole but a free man.

Suzanne was ready. She had packed up everything and had left her car at her brother's place.

We flew immediately to Nelson, landed in Castlegar, British Columbia after a heavy snowfall and drove in a 4x4 to Suzanne's cousin's place.

I didn't have a clue who these cousins were, but Suzanne had talked with them previously.

Nelson was amazing. They couldn't have released me in a better place in the whole world. It was a beautiful town. Her cousin had an old house on the ranch built with reclaimed materials. The furnace was a 45-gallon drum with a pipe going out of it. The kitchen had a wood stove.

They had a big 4x4 vehicle that ploughed right through the snow. You had to drive a 4x4 to get there. You could not access it any other way, except by walking.

We were the second highest house on the mountain. It had floor-to-ceiling windows that overlooked the town of Nelson below – really beautiful at night with the lights below.

Holy shit! Just think about being in the mountains! I felt I was living a life of luxury. In prison – no TVs in cells. I was limited to watching TV only on Saturdays for an hour in the yard – on a tiny TV mounted in a wooden box. Now I could watch whenever I wanted.

We had a mattress on the floor in the living room that was part of the kitchen. The room was square, with 6-foot windows. You could see the lights from the town and the river running through the town. We were surrounded by mountains. It was a dream-like place for me. I was in awe of its beauty. For ten years, I had not seen even one tree root. Now I was living in a forest with millions of trees.

When you are in prison, you can't see the tree roots, you can only see the tops of the trees above the fence. You don't look up at the sky because, if you did, you would go crazy. When you look at the fence, you think about jumping it.

Sometimes I just wanted to jump the fence and have them shoot at me. I was an extremist before. My life meant nothing to me. When you have nothing in life, you want nothing and then they can't control you. It's that simple.

The first time in my life I wanted something was when I met Suzanne. Before that, when I was in prison, I hated the world and I believed that the world hated me in return. My attitude was, "Don't try to get me to soften up because of your fuckin' visit. Keep your garbage away from me." I never had a visit for 15 years.

The more you become immune the tougher you become. You get used to it. I didn't even miss visitors after a while. I won't be a soft kid because you want to give me candy – you don't trust anybody – I didn't want their candy because I didn't trust them....

I wasn't used to visiting in a small town, I didn't even have a parole officer. They told me to go to the police station. At the police station, they said, "Listen, we don't have time for you to report to us. We know you reported today. You are in Nelson and life is good here. See you later."

My god, they gave me parole and I didn't have to report even one single day! We lived in Nelson for six months, from December 16, 1981 to July 1, 1982.

They were all hippies. Suzanne's cousin had a good job as an electrician. He also had chickens and four pigs. They were going to Manitoba for a month and asked us to take care of the place.

I replied, "Holy fuck, you bet I will take care of it." I had never seen a chicken before, except on my plate -- so he showed me how to collect the eggs. It was mind boggling.

One afternoon I had a real adventure. Two of the pigs escaped up the mountain. I had to run after them. Fortunately, I was in good shape. I put a cable around one pig and tried to pull him down. You can't get a pig to do anything he doesn't want to do. I finally succeeded in getting the pigs back into the enclosure and gave them a little bit of fruit. Suzanne wondered what the hell was going on.

She was laughing, "Rene is running." If I hadn't been in shape, I would have died that day. I picked up those two pigs, locked them in and redid the enclosure to make sure they didn't escape again.

Imagine! We spent a month living that life – just like in the movies.

Then I found a job. I went downtown to a hotel where the guy was looking for a cook. When I walked in, he said he really needed a chef – not a cook. It was a tourist hotel in a skiing area.

The guy said, "I need a chef." I replied, "I am a chef." He hired me.

I was a good baker, could cut meat and cook it, but I was definitely not a chef. There were two women working there – an older one and a younger one, in her 20s. The younger woman was an Italian and a good cook.

I had no choice but to lean on her. I said, "Listen, I am going to give you a raise, but you will work with me every day. You will make sure that the staff do what they are supposed to do and you will teach me at the same time."

She was really nice and agreed to that. I started to do the pastry there, and then I hired my wife's cousin – who was a fantastic baker. She took over all the pastry making – I was so pleased.

Being a chef in a hotel meant setting up the menu, running the restaurant, and being in charge of 30 staff. I wasn't experienced in any of that, but I was good with people – and I managed them. I never abused people – never rude – people liked me and wanted to do the job with me and taught me.

And then I started to learn the movements of the staff. I found out that the night chef was a drunk. I said, "I am going to deal with him." And I talked him into not drinking on the job.

Suzanne and I got married, January 23, 1981. We didn't have many guests at the wedding – just four. Her cousins and another couple.

We started the wedding by walking from our house to the hotel.

Every time you walk, you don't even get tired, because you turn around and you see the city and the lights everywhere.

The cook that night did Cornish hens for us. Everyone had wine to drink, except me, because I don't drink.

The night we got married, Suzanne picked up the phone and called her mom. "Mom, we just got married – Rene and I." Suzanne was 30 years old – it was as if she was only 19 and getting married.

I didn't have anyone to call with our news.

Back at the hotel, I spoke to the owner and said, "Look at everything we have done. Will you give me a raise?"

He replied, "Yes, I will give you 50 cents."

I said, "You know what? I think you need the money more than I do. I quit."

I applied to work for the Town of Nelson and they hired me. I got a job as a laborer for the city of Nelson – building sidewalks.

In this town, nobody was in a hurry. Nobody rushed to do things. You would take an hour and a half for lunch.

When there was work to be done, we did it and gave up our lunch. When there was no work, we puttered around.

We moved into the town, rented a place in mid-town close to work – a small, small house. It was now March. The windows were open all over the place in the house. There was an old woman who lived next to us. She was about 85 or 86 years old. I started to help her do the garden. Suzanne liked gardening too. One day she came to us and said, "Have this on my behalf." She gave us the most delicious borscht I have ever tasted. It was an old Russian recipe, made with tomatoes and beets.

We had the time of our lives in that house. I had a good job. Suzanne didn't need to work. Our expenses were not large – the rent was almost nothing. The house was maybe 500 square feet. The bathroom had a shower and a sink. There was a kitchen. You had to climb up a bit to get into the bed. The ceiling had a trap door with stairs that pulled down but there was nothing up there. When you are in love and you are together, you are happy to have 500 square feet – you don't need 1,500.

When we first moved to B.C., we didn't have a car. Sometime later Suzanne's father gave us his old 1968 Dodge Monaco. Suzanne's brother put a new motor in it and drove it out to us in B.C. It ran amazingly well after it was fixed up.

We enjoyed life there, although it was stressful for Suzanne. She was used to the flat plains of Manitoba and suddenly she was in the middle of the Rockies in British Columbia where you don't see the sun at all after two o'clock in the afternoon.

Soon after that, Suzanne said, "We have to leave B.C. I'm sorry, but I can't live here anymore. I am too stressed out. I am glad we came here but the mountains make me claustrophobic."

I was surprised but I said. "It's OK. Where do you want to go?"

"I would like to go to Winnipeg."

I didn't like the sound of the name "Winnipeg." I didn't know Winnipeg from a hole in the ground – except for the prison.

When we moved back to Winnipeg, we drove that big Dodge Monaco. We stopped at the bypass at the start of the Okanagan Valley. This is July 1 now – and it was snowing! We stopped there, got out of the car and threw snowballs at each other. Then we kept on driving to Winnipeg.

We moved to Winnipeg in July 1981. Once again, we were living in the little house on Hindley Street. I always joked about this. Just the other week Suzanne mentioned it. "I would like to see the house." When we drove by, I said, "Look. Your little house on the Hindley." This was the same house where Suzanne had lived before we went to B.C. Her brother had rented it for the six months we lived in Nelson. He was still living there when we came back but all the furniture was Suzanne's. Her brother found a new place and moved out.

I went to work for New Flyer Industries. I lasted for only two days. I was building buses and doing insulation – drilling parts. I was bored…. I quit right away but I needed money.

I had started seeing my partner again, who was also in Winnipeg. We got a gun and robbed one of the larger department stores. We got $15,000 or so – an amount that would keep me going for a while.

Then I said to Suzanne, "Listen, Suzanne. I don't want to live in Winnipeg. I want to leave. I hate Winnipeg. I don't know why, but I don't like Winnipeg."

She asked, "Where do you want to go?"

"Why don't we move to Edmonton? It's booming. There's lots of work there."

"OK. If you want to go, we will go."

So, we moved to Edmonton. I found a job right away in construction. Things were booming. I was working in Fort Saskatchewan for a huge chemical company. My job was to direct the trucks when they were dropping off the dirt or other materials. It was an oil plant, but they were also making lots of chemicals.

Even in Edmonton, I was robbing on the side.

About one o'clock in the afternoon, we committed the big robbery. I drove like crazy – right downtown to the main street.

I purposely drove my car right into a bus that was lined up there with all the other buses. The bus drivers were all reporting in upstairs. Because we had been carefully checking out their routines for some time, we knew that they parked their buses and then were in the office for 15 to 20 minutes before they came back down. I went right upstairs and said, "Listen, sir, I don't know who the driver is for that bus, but 15 minutes ago I drove into your bus by accident."

They wrote in their report that Mr. Rene Durocher drove his car into the bus at 1:00 p.m. So I had my alibi. How could I be driving my car into the bus at 1:00 p.m. and also robbing the Brinks guy at 1:00 p.m.? My experience was making me smarter.

We had planned it out carefully. Nobody but me could know the exact time I ran into the bus. It was probably 1:15. For the bus driver and everybody in the office upstairs, it was 1:00 because I was waiting. I said, "I ran into a bus by accident 15 minutes ago, at 1:00 p.m."

The bus driver said, "Yes. It must have been 1:00 because I was on my way out."

The bus driver went down and checked the bus. "There's no damage."

"I know. But I didn't want to hit it and then run off. I'm sorry."

So I played the part of the nice guy who did the right thing and reported an accident.

We got a good $200,000 from robbing that truck. You can hide the money anywhere you want. There are lots of hiding places. I don't remember where I put it – probably in the trunk of my big Dodge Monaco. It was as big as a boat. When the Brinks trucks pick up money, there is only one bag. You can put $100,000 to $200,000 in a bag about the size of a duffle bag."

Suzanne didn't know that I was robbing stores again. If she had known, it would have been the end – the end of everything.

That's what hurt her the most. I did things and always managed to hide them from her. I never deposited the money in a bank account. I just told her, "I got a job for a couple of days." I always had cash. I didn't even have a bank account. It's easy to keep money if you have only $5,000 or so. You can keep it in your pockets. She trusted me. She would never have thought in a million years that I would rob that department store. It's always easy to hide something from someone who loves you and wants to believe in you. She loved me and wanted to believe in me.

When things were getting uncomfortable, I asked Suzanne if we could move.

So, we moved again - this time to Montreal.

CHAPTER TEN
Two Million Dollars

We were going to start afresh in Montreal.

I bought my first house, on the small street, nice street, nice neighborhood. By this time, we had two children. My son Daniel, who we called Dan, and my daughter who we always called Mel – I guess I wanted shortcuts to call them.

And then we are there, I have a nice life.

I was feeling the need to settle, to look after my family, but did not have the skills to make it on the outside world. I had wanted to change but couldn't.

The pressure became too big. I was where it all started.

I was back in Montreal for the first time in my life since I was a kid. I remembered how I robbed – except things were different now, the banks there were untouchable. So were Brinks trucks since the cops were following them left and right.

There was no way to rob a bank in Montreal anymore. Because of the insurance policies, the tills contained only $1,500. What can you do with $1,500? You certainly don't have time to empty ten tills. So you forget the Montreal banks. With an old partner of mine, we drove to Toronto to look for bigger opportunities and started following Brinks trucks.

With another partner I decided to buy into a Mascot company together. Mascots were very popular in the 80s and we made the big heads for the mascots. We did festivals with Smurfs or Santas. We had five or six Santa suits that people could rent. It was a small costume company. The important thing for us was that this kind of company was allowed to buy liquid rubber. With liquid rubber you could make masks.

But our plans were to hit Toronto for the big money. The Mascot company was all part of my plan for the Toronto job. I didn't want to be recognized by anyone. So, I made rubber masks for myself in the shop. I always disguised myself when we went to Toronto. Sometimes I wore a mask, with a beard and a wig. Some of those wigs cost $400 or $500. We would drive to Ottawa, park the car there and rent a car with Ontario licence plates. We didn't want to be driving around Toronto with Quebec licence plates.

I told Suzanne that I had a jeans company and that I had to travel across Quebec frequently to sell the jeans. Our registered brand name was Vendetti and the jeans were made in La Beauce just outside Montreal. Lots of stores were selling jeans but they all wanted credit – with 60 days to pay. If you wanted to sell your jeans, you had to give them credit. Lots of them didn't pay. They went bankrupt, but I didn't care.

Meanwhile, I was going to Toronto, following Brinks truck after Brinks truck -- planning the big job. In Toronto, we checked out all the downtown buildings. We followed lots of Brinks trucks. You never follow the same one. You follow one guy until he finishes his run. Then you know his route.

Once you know the run, you don't follow him anymore – you go ahead of him. When the truck gets to the first place, you are already there. Then you leave right away. When they get to the second place, you are already there. You always get there before them because they always follow the same route. They don't have a choice because the company wants to save money on gas. All this information was in our heads. We never wrote anything down.

We would follow several trucks and then make our decision about which one to rob. Some routes weren't good because they delivered new money. You never steal new money because it is all marked.

Something like this takes planning.

For one thing, you always have two cars. You never follow a Brinks truck with just one car, because they are trained to continuously look out the back of the vehicle. If they see the same car, they know you are following them as they do their run. So, we always had two rental cars – one for me and one for my partner. We would follow the truck with one taking the lead and the other one behind. Then he would pass me and take the lead. We applied the knowledge we had gained from robbing banks to robbing Brinks trucks.

Brinks routes are like milk runs. The trucks have to be on time and they arrive at the same time each day. The store prepares the bag of money. The bag is ready and the driver just has to sign and go.

Now it was a new adventure – we decided we weren't going to rob the truck but we were going to rob the guy. We did a lot of preparation to see what his routines were. We would sit in the car or in the mall and watch the guy – going in, coming out. We picked the big stores.

My partner would go in, and then about ten seconds later, the guy would sign and come out with the bag. We had on balaclavas and tuques, walked into the store and hid in the racks of clothes. I had watched this guy so much I knew he was as regular as clockwork. He always took the same path, with the same number of steps. There were four exits in the store. The truck was parked outside.

We were already inside. My partner was right there because he would be the first one out. He was the driver – a great getaway driver. I was the action guy. When the Brinks guy walked by me, I put the gun to his back and said, "If you move, you are dead." Then I took his gun and said, "Give me the bag. Get out." He went out through one set of doors; we went out through another.

It worked.

After focussing on Toronto and following the Brinks trucks for quite a while, we found two jobs that we really wanted to do. Then the Brinks company went on strike. It was 1985. My partner said, "Why don't we check out Vancouver?"

We drove to Vancouver. I didn't feel comfortable. It wasn't a good city with all the bridges. I said, "No. I like Toronto." We came to the same conclusion that we both liked Toronto.

However, we were starting to argue all the time. We would spend two or three days in Toronto. Sometimes we would travel there two or three days in a row and we would argue all the time. I always wore a different disguise. I would put on another beard or a different wig. I always wore a hat. I was very professional in the way I prepared. I made myself a jacket like the DHL Delivery Company by printing out their logo and putting it on my jacket.

One day I went to check on Adelaide Street.

I looked like a regular delivery guy with my pad and package –in my DHL company jacket and hat -- and I went to the Toronto Stock Exchange.

I got on the elevator with the Brinks guys and went down. They were going to pick up $400,000,000 or $500,000,000 in investment certificates. I said to my partner, "We should rob that fuckin' truck. If they ever arrest us, we can make a deal – an exchange. Let us go and you can have your investment certificates." They were worth $400,000,000 or $500,000,000 on the Stock Exchange.

I went down on the elevator with the Brinks guys and followed them into the tunnel.

I asked them politely, "Do you want me to help you hold the bag?" They replied, "No, thank you, sir." I was really good at talking to people – just a friendly guy. I wasn't aggressive at all. My god, I was on my best behavior.

The Brinks guys went into the vault. I looked outside the vault, and I looked at them and I went into the vault. Imagine -- I was in the same building as the stock exchange –following the guys going into the vault.

I said I was delivering a package for X.

I saw them unload the paper stocks worth $400,000,000 or $500,000,000. If I had been prepared I could have gotten in the elevator with them – go to the underground parking lot and hold a gun to their heads and get the stocks. It would have been the perfect job. I could have retired with that money.

The guy asked me, "What do you want?"

"I am with DHL and I am looking for this address."

When I gave him the address, he told me it was across the street.

"Oh, I am sorry. I would have never…"

"It's OK. Mistakes happen."

"I'll go across the street and deliver my package. I'll leave you to your job."

I returned to my partner and said, "We should rob them. This is the best opportunity to cover our asses. If they arrest us, we would be home free."

Get the two guys and bury the money for two or three years. Then blackmail them. Talk to our lawyer – use the privileged client-lawyer information. It could take years to locate the stocks.

My partner refused. "No. No."

We were getting mad at each other. I almost hit him.

By this time, I didn't see myself as a thug. I saw myself as a professional. I prided myself on my work. Becoming a criminal is like learning a trade and doing an apprenticeship, just like a plumber. I learned by robbing small places, doing break and enters, then stealing TVs from store windows. You build yourself up to do bigger things. I knew there were bigger things out there to do than robbing a small corner store. This is where I had started as a child.

You have to become good at your job, because you could end up in jail every time you commit a crime. The more careful you are, the better the job you will do. If you rush, you are done.

Rushing makes you nervous. I never used drugs. I never drank. It was like a baseball game. You go over it all the night before to make sure you have everything covered. You control everything possible.

The only thing you cannot control is damn probability. You can't totally control what happens when you knock on the door. So, the night before a job, my partner would sleep in my other bedroom. We didn't go anywhere. No booze. Nothing.

I was even helping others plan other robberies. I did so much research I could hand it off to others. There was one plan that went well. Their take was $2,000,000 or $3,000,000 and I got only $65,000. I should have gotten $1,000,000. "A crook is a crook."

Three days after we got back from Vancouver, we went back to Toronto.

The first thing we saw when we parked was a money truck. "Look at that fuckin' truck." I knew where he was going to finish his day – where he always finished. The train and the subway station were there. There was a place on the main floor where they brought all the money collected during the day. The guy was parked right at the corner of Yonge and Bloor.

It was OK because we had a third guy with us that day. I'll always regret it – not because he did something wrong but because he didn't do anything.

The company's name was Cache. They had been hired to do the Brinks' runs during the time of the strike. There were no options – money had to be picked up and delivered regularly. It was very lucky for us. When I parked that night, I saw the truck right away. It was like a van but bigger than a regular van, with all the security features.

I had followed the guy before and he always made the same mistake. Because it was so hot and humid in Toronto in the summer, he always rolled the window down a little bit.

I said, "I am going to fuckin' get that guy. He is a dead turkey."

There was no question for me. We were going to do the job. For my partner, it was always, "No. No." at that time.

I said, "Listen. We've been fuckin' coming here for three weeks. Don't wait for Brinks to end the strike. Let's do the job."

"No. I don't want to."

I had become really nervous and anxious, because my money was disappearing fast. I had almost no money left to keep on doing what I was doing.

"Fuck you," I said. "I'll do it by myself."

"You can't fuckin' do it. It's our job."

I said, "Watch me."

I went to the side of the truck and put my gun up to the Cache driver's head – through the window that he always left open a little bit. I said, "If you move, you are dead. Now, you are going to turn off your fuckin' truck and open the door, or I will kill you right here."

He knew I meant business from the way I was talking. The guy opened the door. I jumped on him, handcuffed him, and shoved him into the back of the van. I started the truck and headed down the Gardiner Expressway, then onto the 401 Highway.

The guys were following me as we approached the 401. My partner was fuckin' amazed that I drove the truck, and that I did the job by myself.

The plan was to stop behind the big Holiday Inn on the 401. I went there and backed the truck in on one side.

The whole time I was driving, the guy was screaming, "Please don't kill me." I just said, "Shut the fuck up." I wouldn't kill him. I didn't need to kill him.

But he didn't know that. He was just afraid that I was going to kill him. Sometimes I still hear his voice.

I found out later that this guy had two young kids, that he quit his job the same day and that he was never able to work in that field again. When you start to change your life, you start to hear those sounds, those voices.

But, at that time, I said, "Shut the fuck up. I've got you. What the fuck use are you to me?" It took the cops two hours to get the handcuffs off him. They had to get cutters because I had thrown the key in the garbage.

We dumped the guy there, left him in the van, and took off. I think it took the cops an hour to find the van.

It was July, 1985, I'll never forget it. We went to my partner's apartment and just dumped the bags on the floor.

It was 43 bags!

Two million dollars – a pile of money on the floor about the size of a large dining room table, mostly $20 bills. It was old money!

I just looked at it, thinking, "My god we did it!" What a headrush! I had never seen so much money in a pile before!

We celebrated for one moment. Then, sweating profusely, we started rifling through it – throwing the new bills – the traceable bills – onto a pile to be burned. They were useless to us.

It is the test of every robbery – to divide the loot harmoniously after – to fulfill the crime contract. Not to finish it. Not to finish it completely – leaving everyone satisfied – was to create a deadly leak. And one must do it quickly – before the second thinking can take hold.

It was a successful heist.

By the time the police found the guy in the van, we were already on our way to Montreal. We were well equipped with a scanner in our car to see if there were police anywhere. It was important to keep the gun in case the police arrived. I kept the gun. If we were stopped and the police checked the car, they would have died. There is no doubt in my mind. The police would never have taken the money away from us.

Never in a million years would I have given them the money.

My lifelong ambition had been to pull off a million-dollar heist. I had done it. I was truly the man! All my life – I had suffered the abuse of some authority who had power over me. No one had power over me now! And no one would ever have power over me again!

CHAPTER ELEVEN
Most Wanted

After we split the two million, as I was leaving my partner's apartment, I said to him, "Listen. Our partnership is over. I am going to find somebody else."

Then I went to see Jacques. Jacques and I, we bought a franchise for a Yogi Pet Store – a chain of pet stores in Montreal.

At that time, we were the fifth largest pet store in Canada. Our store was in the west part of Montreal, where people loved their dogs, cats, and birds more than their babies – at least that was our perception. Everywhere you went the English people had frisky dogs. I said that it was the best place to buy a pet store. I knew the president of Hagen was the biggest supplier in Montreal then for pet store supplies.

Everything was marked up 100%. If you bought something for $1.00, like a dog toy, you sold it for $2.19 – 19 cents for the tax. I did things so that parents and kids would be excited to come to the store. I brought in monkeys and birds – something different every week.

I was a good business man. I would give the kids a goldfish in a bag for free. They were so excited. But how would the goldfish live? He couldn't stay in the bag so the mother would have to buy a bowl, some food, other little things. Before you know it, the mom has spent $25 or $30. You make 50% of that – all because you gave away a 49-cent fish to a kid. I was Santa Claus – always giving something away. And it was going well.

We attracted people into the store with unusual animals. We had a little lion, a monkey and birds. The lion was on a chain and people would pat him. The birds were trained to do whatever you wanted them to do.

At that time, I was working 70 or 75 hours a week – starting a business and working seven days a week – staff and payroll. They would have never come to get me.

The only thing I had bought for myself was a 1985 or 1986 Prelude. That's the only money I had spent. I had put the rest of the money into the store, but it was not in my name. It was in the name of my friend, Jacques. We had those two businesses – the mascot store and the pet store. I couldn't just hide that amount of money in my pocket -- so I hid it in the ceiling of my first business with him. He knew about it. You know…. You work with someone. You have a business partnership with him. You trust him.

One day I was in my store and I saw two guys wearing trench coats walk in. Right away, I knew they were cops. Only cops dress like that. I turned around and looked at the back door. There were two more guys covering the back door. By the time they came at me in the store, there were probably six, seven, eight cops, I don't know. They said, "You are under arrest for the Brinks truck robbery in Toronto."

I said, "I've never robbed a fuckin' truck in Toronto. I've never been to Toronto."

I knew he couldn't prove I had been in Toronto. I always went from Montreal to Ottawa, picked up a rental car, drove to Toronto with Ontario plates. No one had written down my license plate number.

But they arrested me and took me to the Parthenais Inmate Centre. They charged me. At that time, I was the only one arrested.

A few days later, they went to get Gilles. I don't know why. He was never involved. A few days later they went to get Real, because they had found his fingerprints on the other job I had given him in Toronto. Then they arrested my partner. I went to court, pleaded not guilty and asked the judge to give me bail. He set bail at $275,000.

Then I called my partner and said, "You have to get me some money. I have some but I need more for my bail." He refused to bail me out. I said, "You son of a bitch. Fuck you all. I will plead guilty."

I ended up with another 15 years, on top of the 16, and on top of the 14 that were still not finished. By the time they counted, I still had 28 years left to serve.

Here I was – a married man, a father of two kids, who suddenly really cared about his wife and kids. I always thought that nothing mattered to the rest of the world. But Suzanne – she just went berserk. I saw her melt. She lost weight and dropped to 118 pounds. She was responsible for two kids and the house, and I was back in jail. I just wanted to die.

Stony Mountain refused to take me. No penitentiary in Quebec wanted me.

They shipped me to the worst shithole – Prince Albert in Saskatchewan. Jimmy O. was the warden there. His name was O'Sullivan, but we all called him Jimmy O. He was a funny guy and a straight shooter. The cops didn't find any money. They thought I had stashed the money somewhere. One day Jimmy O. calls me into his office. "Rene, you are going to have to go to Toronto."

I told him. "No fuckin' way am I going to Toronto. They will kill me."

"You have no choice, and I don't have any choice. I've got a warrant for you. There are cops who will come and pick you up and take you to Toronto to go to court."

"Fuck you."

"No, Rene. If I had a choice, I wouldn't send you."

"I am telling you, Jimmy. They want to kill me."

"Listen. In a couple of days, they will be here, and I don't have a choice."

It is true, when there's a warrant, the warden gets charged if he doesn't agree.

What they didn't know was that I had a few friends in the Prince Albert Penitentiary. Before I left, I said to one of them, "Do you have any cash?" He said, "Yes," and gave me a $20 bill which I stashed.

I was swearing the whole time. They flew me to Toronto. I went to court and refused to testify. I pretended I was sick, and fainted in court.

I was guarded by two cops. They took me to a hotel. The one cop said, "Rene we have a room to sleep."

"No fuckin' way. What do you want from me?"

They didn't say anything.

I knew what they wanted from me. To this day, I swear on my life that they wanted me to get away, escape from them. And they wanted to follow me to see where I had stashed my money. Then they would have killed me and taken the money because these guys were criminals – no better than me. In cities like Toronto or Montreal, you have bad cops, and good cops. You never know which one you're dealing with. Maybe those percentages are too high. Maybe it's 0.5% bad and 99.5% good. But every police force has bad cops. And these two, I knew they were a piece of shit.

I said, "What do you want to do now?"

The cop said, "I need to go home and change because I haven't had a change of clothes for two days. I am going to take you home with me."

"OK."

I started to play the guy and decided to be good. I realized what they had wanted to do with me and that I could wind up dead.

The cop lived on the seventh or eighth floor. We went up the elevator and into his apartment. I could see the living room, the kitchen.

He said, "Rene, just sit here and have a coffee. I'm going to take a quick shower."

"OK. I'll wait for you."

He went into the shower. About 30 or 40 seconds later, he came out and said, "Oh, Rene. Are you OK? You have your coffee. Do you need anything else?"

I knew that he wanted to check to see if I was doing anything.

He went back in. I listened carefully. I could hear the shower. He undressed and went into the shower. Immediately I left the apartment. I didn't take the elevator. I just ran down the seven or eight floors and out onto the street. I crossed the street, but I didn't have a clue where I was. It was in the new part of town. I saw a bus and jumped on. I had my $20 bill. I said to the bus driver, "I just have this."

He replied, "Go sit down." In a city like Toronto, they don't want to change a $20 bill – at least they didn't back then. Here I am – sitting on the bus. I can hear helicopters all around me. I'm sure the cop called it in as soon as he got out of the shower and realized that I had escaped. But they were looking for someone on foot. I was so lucky that the bus was coming just when I ran out of the building. I was still in good shape. They wouldn't think that I had time to run and hop on a bus. I took the city bus to end of the line and then started to hitchhike.

At the end of the line, I went into a convenience store, and I saw these people who were speaking French. I said to them, "Listen, guys, I was smacked over the head last night in Toronto. They stole my wallet and I have nothing. I live in Montreal. Can you give me a ride?"

And the guy said, "Sure, I am going there right now. I am from there."

So, I sat in the back seat of the big Cadillac. The guy, with his wife up front, drove me right to Montreal.

I arrived in Montreal the same evening but they were looking for me all over Toronto. They spent a million dollars on that investigation trying to find me. When I got to Montreal, I called my friend.

My friend already knew that I had escaped and that I was the "most wanted" person in Canada. It was all over the news right across the country.

Those cops were now scrambling to cover their asses. The story they were telling was: "This guy was sitting in my car and pretended to be sick. Because I wanted to be good to him and help him, I took off the handcuffs, and let him throw up. He started to run and then he escaped." He told the media, his boss – everyone – this story.

I was mad as hell because I am sure they would have killed me if I had not escaped the way I did. There is no doubt in my mind.

They thought they could have put their hands on one-third of $2,000,000. There wasn't that amount left then because I had already bought the store and the inventory with part of my share. Then they would have killed me and they could have retired with my money. I was so mad. I thought to myself, "Now I'll get them." You can't imagine how happy

I was. I was laughing at him. That cop was a fuckin' idiot. I hurt them when they were trying to hurt me.

But now I needed to get out of the country.

In those days in Quebec all the birth certificates were issued by the priest in the parish where you were born. I said to my friend, "Go and tell the priest you've been smacked over the head and that they stole your wallet and identification."

The next day my friend came and said, "Hey Rene, here is the birth certificate." It was someone else's – a person I didn't know.

I want you to do something else for me. I told him. "There is a guy who owes me $5,000 – Richard. Call him and tell him I need the money. He got me the money."

Then I went to a federal government office. I said, "Listen. I got robbed – my wallet and everything. The only thing I have is my birth certificate that I got from the church yesterday. I need to get a social insurance card."

"We'll give you the same social insurance number as you had before."

"I don't remember what it was."

So they wrote the number down on a piece of paper for me.

"We'll mail the card to you in a few days."

I gave them an address in Montreal.

Then I went to the office to get a driver's license. In those days there weren't photos on the licenses. So, I gave them the same story and they gave me a driver's license – all legal – with someone else's name who didn't have a criminal record. The guy was alive at the time and never knew that I was using his name. I used it for a long time and I don't think he ever knew. And it was all because my friend got somebody else's birth certificate.

With my new identity, birth certificate, social insurance number and driver's license, I said to myself, "Let's get the hell out of here." I went to downtown Montreal and took a bus to Atlantic City. Atlantic City is the place where Donald Trump built all those casinos. Lots of Quebeckers go there or to Plattsburg to play bingo. I remember, as a kid, my mom used to take us to play bingo in Plattsburg when she went there with her aunt. We drove down in the car. When we were young, it was so exciting to go to the States.

When the bus reached the border, the guy asked, "Where are you going?"

"To Atlantic City to gamble."

"Oh, we have some really nice casinos there."

"That's where I'm going."

But as soon as I reached New York, I got off the bus. I took a plane to Florida. It was my first time in Florida. I rented a car in Florida – but not from a company. I rented a car from a guy who had two or three cars for rent. I paid him in cash.

Then right away I got myself a 57 Magnum. I wanted to have a gun immediately. In the States you can buy a gun as easily as you can buy a pound of butter.

That's when I learned that my business partner, who was my front for the store, went into my stash, didn't manage the store well and went bankrupt. We lost everything.

I went to live at a motel called La Vie en Rose. There was a singer from Quebec there – Johnny Farago.

Here I was in the motel in Florida, listening to his music, and, all the while, in Toronto, in Montreal, all over Canada they were looking for me. I was the "most wanted" man in Canada.

I returned to Canada about two weeks later, angry and vengeful, and reconnected with Suzanne. She convinced me to surrender.

I threw my gun in the river and went to *Fifth Estate,* a Canadian television program, and surrendered there – the only safe place I could trust and told them the entire story. I was then returned to the Saskatchewan federal penitentiary -- the Prince Albert Correctional Centre.

CHAPTER TWELVE
Good Behavior

While I was serving time in Prince Albert, Suzanne came to visit me with the two kids. She had driven the entire way – 14 hours. She gave me an ultimatum – and I knew she meant it.

Suzanne said, "Rene, I can't let our kids be raised this way, with what you are doing with your life. I'm going away." And I knew this time she was serious.

I knew that once she made up her mind – she would go through with it.

I told her, "I'll do better. I will change."

It was a big decision. I had to leave my hate and choose love.

But in my own mind, I had no idea how I was going to even accomplish that.

How can you change when you don't know what you have to change? I had survived on my hatred that was directed to my father as I was growing up.

How can you change when you don't know what is wrong with you? When you think that you are right and that it's the other people who are wrong?

My mindset was that I was okay. I thought I would change if I had money. "If I have money, I won't rob a bank."

I didn't realize that there are people who don't have money who don't rob banks. It's the way I perceived myself. Banks only meant money. Trucks meant money. I always found reasons to justify myself, to think that I was right.

Then I looked at myself and said, " I will lose my kids." I hated my father my whole life. It is confusing even for an adult. I didn't understand what was going on. I just knew that I had lost someone I loved.

And here I am locked up in Prince Albert, with another 28 years left.

I grew up destroying myself. I was my own worst enemy because I was involved with self-destruction. It was how I ran my life.

I realized that if I had truly loved Suzanne that much, I would not have done the robbery.

I always had a reason for doing things, but I didn't think that other people had a reason to walk out on me. I felt sorry for myself – "Poor me. Poor me." Somebody had walked out on me. When I started to really look at this, I said, "What the heck can I do to change that?" I didn't know.

Whenever I met a psychologist or shrink, I'd tell them to go to hell, that they were no good for me. Nobody was good for me. I was the only one that was good for anything I wanted to do.

It was my hatred towards my father. I always said I would never be like him and, if I had kids, I would never walk away from them.

It was a shock to realize I had walked away from my kids. I was the same as him.

After Suzanne left, I started a correspondence course in marketing and administration from Athabasca University. I changed and I didn't get into trouble anymore. I was doing very well, and my goal was to go to transfer to Stony Mountain, to be close to Suzanne and the kids.

Then I applied for a transfer. They turned me down the first time. I reapplied again a year later. For the first time in my life, I was in prison and not getting into fights, not getting into any kind of violence. The first time in my life. It had never happened to me before. I was keeping away from everyone who was violent.

Slowly I began to change. At first it was simply protecting myself by staying away from everyone. I did this because I would not get into an argument, I would not feel like taking anyone's head off. I just did my own thing and worked in the kitchen. Finally, they agreed that I could move to Stony. I had gone for almost two years without seeing my kids.

I exhibited good behavior – self-protecting behavior. I made lifestyle changes. All the time I was wondering what would happen if someone pushed me too far. Would I blow? When would I blow? It was like living on a tightrope. I was always watching myself, watching everyone and everything, watching where I was going and avoiding everyone else. Then they agreed to move me back to Stony.

I called Suzanne. "I have been transferred to Stony. Would you come and visit me?'"

When she came to visit me, I said, "Suzanne, I don't know what to do."

The first thing I did was give her access to my file if she wanted. Then the Parole Officer sat down with Suzanne and discussed with her if I had made any progress over the past two years – using his file. After that Suzanne started visiting me again.

That's when I started to see Dr. Richard Howes, the psychologist at Stony. He was excellent for me, except that I kept hiding my deepest secret, because I didn't know how to talk about it. I didn't have a clue. When I had not been wrong for 40 years, how could I be wrong now?

We had good meetings and I talked about some stuff, but I never told him about the sexual abuse. I believe this was the part of my life that caused me to live the way I did but I can't blame it on that. Some kids who have been abused don't turn to a life of crime. Maybe they are screwed-up but they don't do the kinds of things that I did. Sometimes I get angry about that.

I began to work with Dr. Howes.

That's the way it went for me – the real change. Suzanne kept visiting me every week after that. It was a slow learning, through telling my story and with Dr. Howes starting to open the doors. I started to tell my story over and over again, and that was my healing.

And because I learned the importance of telling my story, I also got other people to open up and tell their stories.

I know the story of every one of my clients. I didn't write anything down. It's all in my head but I could relate to any of their stories. I was so caught up in this.

So, I basically began my real change, because of my fear of losing my family.

I had to let go of my memories and my hatred. I hated my father for leaving us and running away when I was young. I was raised like that.

It was a process that took years. Change didn't come because of one major incident that led me to ask myself, "What am I going to do with my life now?"

It is a life process.

We make mistakes all our lives – I still made mistakes, but I never committed another robbery. I started step by step. I couldn't stop doing one thing and not deal with another. It's not possible.

For one thing, even though I was seeing Dr. Howes, I never told him about the abuse of the priests – I wasn't ready to acknowledge that. So even as I was changing there were still a hidden darkness. And for us to change completely, I had to open up completely.

Psychologists don't have a crystal ball. Psychologists are only as good as the information you provide them with. Dr. Howes was good but I did not provide him with all the information. I was afraid and ashamed and maybe even unaware.

I never wanted to talk about anything that happened to me. It is funny. I got to the point where I wanted to change, but I had to be careful that I didn't make it a story. For me it was not the story that changed – it was the process, but the process did involve a lot of storytelling – oh my god, yes.

I started listening to the stories inside… of the guys inside – and they opened up to me. I really listened… I understood. I think their stories helped me.

It is funny because, after I started to work at Stony, I would go and talk with Dr. Howes about my clients. The amazing thing is – I became good friends with people I had despised. I worked with them and became good friends with them.

But when I was still in jail, I kept meeting with Dr. Howes, and then I started the work release program. He was one of my speakers. I had a speaker every week – like Dr. Howes and the warden. They would all speak at my program. All the guys had to participate. There was no free ride. Everyone had to take the wheel of the bus and drive it for one week. No one was allowed to be a passenger. I would give each guy an essay to do – an assignment to talk about. Because of that, the program became real and truthful. I involved the staff, the guards – whoever wanted to come. No one ever turned me down when they were invited. Everyone came to the group meetings.

In 1991, I went to Graham Reddoch, then Executive Director of the John Howard Society, to help with a program called *Stonewall Quarry Work Program* – a kind of community work program.

In this program, inmates were encouraged to go out into the tiny town of Stonewall, right next to the institution, to work at something – anything – that would show "good will" to the community and hopefully change their attitudes towards us – realizing that we were humans and not some kind of animal, monster, or whatever image they were projecting onto us. By doing good things in a small community and in small ways, the programmers hoped to start to change public opinion.

Then the warden took notice. And when a volunteer position opened up to work in Quarry Park in Stonewall as a volunteer, Art Makujt said to me, "I am the Warden here. I want you to apply."

I did it. I applied.

Then I met Mark Grindley. We met when I spoke to the Town of Stonewall the first time about how I had created a program at Stony for work release in the Stonewall Quarry. Mark came to hear the speech and then he asked me if I would be willing to speak at the school. He escorted me the first time I went to the school. Then he escorted me a couple of times to schools in the neighborhoods where he was living. When I got out of prison, I created the Accent on Youth program and then I went to the John Howard Society.

This ended when I was released December 16, 1991, on parole. Suzanne and I moved to the small community of St-Pierre-Jolys, less than 30 minutes south of Winnipeg's Perimeter Highway.

It was perfect for our small family, my wife Suzanne, and my two children. The town was considered affordable, safe, and a place where neighbors still look out for one another – "Where your grocer knew your name."

CHAPTER THIRTEEN
Merchant of Hope

I still think my biggest achievement was my work as an In-Reach worker for the national Life Line program.

This program began when they got rid of the death penalty in 1976. Doing away with capital punishment meant that the prisons were starting to fill up with Lifers. In 1999 there were about 3,442 offenders serving life sentences, about one third of whom are on lifetime parole supervision in the community.

It was John Braithwaite, the former Deputy Commissioner of Communication for the Correctional Service of Canada. He saw the problem. First of all he knew that the Lifers were different than the rest of the population. Most of them had killed in a fit of rage and were probably drunk or stoned out of their mind. They had no intention to kill so they had no skills on how to fight and how to survive the prison. He also realized that, because they had to spend longer than usual in prison, they would have to learn to live together as a group – have a peer support group.

He envisioned the Life Line Program which had three components: In-reach worker with the inmates, community programming, and public awareness.

I could do all of these. I could work on the inside – and I could tell my story.

But John didn't want me in the program. I wasn't a Lifer. This was a program for people who had murdered someone so there was some resistance to my being hired, because I wasn't in prison for a murder. I was violent – but I wasn't a murderer.

It was because of the influence of Art Makujt, the warden at Stony, that I was even considered for the position.

He said to John and the other organizers, "If you want Life Line in my prison, I'll tell you who you will hire. Rene is the only guy I can trust to come back into my jail. If you don't hire him, we'll just walk away from the program."

That was very powerful for the warden to say that. Art had seen the way I worked with the groups inside. I had kicked some people out of groups because they were trying to play games with me. I was a straight shooter in prison. I would say to the guys in all the groups, "If you don't like it, come and see me." There aren't too many people who can do that in a prison.

Finally, Skip Graham, the creator of Life Line together with Tom French, and John Braithwaite, came to Stony for a meeting.

Three or four months later, Art called me back and said, "Rene, there is a possible job opening at Stony for Life Line."

It was a miracle.

This was pretty great validation of what I was doing from the warden, who had helped me to be released. It was a huge encouragement to me to keep on the path that I had started in jail, turning my life around.

Tom French was the first In-Reach worker, back in 1991. He was a former biker who was a diabetic, and was confined to a wheelchair as a result of a motorcycle accident. Tom started with Millhaven Institution. This was a good place to start because Millhaven is where lifers come into prison in Ontario. Many of them are in shock and put on suicide watch.

Lifers want to take a sleeping pill for the next 15 or 25 years to escape their lengthy sentences.

French thought of his job as keeping lifers "alive, sane, and out of trouble."

I told Tom from the beginning. "You know what? I am always going to appreciate the training you have provided for me. But there are some things I know personally because I've been on the inside. I, as an inmate, am particularly suited to help my fellow inmates to see the truth about their life, to see the impact of their crime. Because I've changed, I can also help them to try to change their life."

I went to Kingston for training, and then I returned to Winnipeg, and I began to work at Stony Mountain Institution as an official In-Reach worker.

When I started, I was so committed I worked around the clock. I was in prison twelve or thirteen hours a day. The warden once said, "Rene, get the hell out of here. You have to take time with your family."

But for me it was not just a job, it was like a mission. I saw myself as a merchant of hope.

Even at home, everything was set up to work from my house. I had my computer at home, and a telephone system that allowed me to hook up with the inmates at a moment's notice. I let them all know that if they were desperate – to call me before they did something wrong. I told that to every one of my clients. "Call me anytime of the night." I had permission from the warden to hand out my telephone number on all the ranges. Every inmate could call me on my 800 number because I was their last line of defense, if I can use that term.

Lots of these guys who gave up on life were really dangerous to themselves and others. So, for me, I wanted to let them know that I was available. I begged them, "Give me a chance to talk to you. If you want to do something, I will not stop you. Just give me a chance to talk to you and, if I can't help you, I will let you go and do what you want."

But I knew that if I could get the fellow into my office, he would never get out of there before I was finished with him the way I wanted him to be. No one ever did anything drastic after spending one hour, five hours or whatever with me. The time didn't matter. I spent whatever time I needed with a guy to make sure he was okay.

The best example I have is a young man whose name was Michael. I had gone to speak at his school. And I remember that there were two kids sitting at the back of the class. They were laughing, and having a good time when I was speaking. They were 15 years old. Before I left, I said to a teacher, "These two kids are going to be in trouble before too long."

It wasn't long after that Michael killed the other kid over a drug deal they had made. Mike was born a drug addict. His dad and his mom were addicted to heroin, or whatever drug they were using.

Michael was sentenced to life seven – and he was only 16 years old.

But when he was serving his time in prison, he made a bomb. He was so smart. He wanted to escape.

The deputy warden of Stony Mountain approached me.

He said, "Rene, one of your clients has made a bomb."

I couldn't believe it. I said, "Come on."

"Yes," he said. "The prison is in lockdown. You have to try to find out what is wrong with this kid." And he gave me his name.

I said, "Holy fuck!" I knew this kid was capable of doing this, because he was always talking about the war, Hitler…. He was fascinated with power and the wars. I knew the institution was in real danger…. I thought of all the inmates, the staff, the harm.

It was about 11:30 at lunch when I called him into my office. He came. It was highly irregular to do this kind of thing, but the word was out. "Let Rene call him whenever he wants. Let him do the job he's got to do."

Once he was in my office, I said, "Mike, the prison is in lockdown. I am told that you built a bomb, and you are on your way to the SHU."

The SHU, the Special Handling Unit, it is the most secure unit. There is one in Prince Albert and one in Quebec. By that time Prince Albert was to be closed and Michael would have been shipped to the SHU in Quebec.

I told the kid, "The prison is going to be in lockdown, which means the other inmates will not be able to have visiting hours, nothing, until this is resolved. If you have something to do with this, you can talk to me. I promise you one thing - I am going to do whatever it takes to help you. But first you are going to help yourself, and you are going to have to help me and the institution. You need to tell us where this bomb is, because they believe that you have made the bomb and now it is up to you, if you want to talk to me. They know you made it, and they are going to search the prison for as long as it takes. They don't care how long it takes or what they have to do.... they are going to do it."

He started telling me the story. Yes, he said, he had made the pipe bomb, in several pieces, and had hidden them in the ceiling of the shop in four different places.

I asked, "Why did you make that bomb?"

He said, "I wanted to jump the fence and when they tried to get me, I would have blown myself up."

"With a bomb?" I asked.

"It would be attached to my chest," he said.

I said, "You realize that the guards in the compound will jump on you, grab you, and pull you off the fence. You would probably kill one of them."

He said, "No, I don't want to do that."

"If you did what you planned, that is exactly what could have happened. They could have died because of your actions in trying to escape."

He said, "I don't want to do that. You can go tell the warden all that stuff."

I said, "No, I am not going to tell the warden your story."

I said this because I knew that, with any inmate in prison, you could never tell him what to do. You only made suggestions as to what he might want to do. You let them twist in their own decision making, until they make the final decision. Because if you tell them what to do and it works you are a hero; but if you tell them what to do and it doesn't work, then you are to blame for everything until the end of the world.

I said, "You do what you are supposed to do. I will be there to support you. No other way around."

He said, "OK."

I called the deputy warden.

I said, "I have some news for you."

He said, "Come to my office right away."

It was a real odd feeling to have such freedom – the run of the entire place – when, just a few years prior, I had been a prisoner behind bars. But, somehow, I had gained the trust of the staff, the warden and also the inmates. I was no longer an inmate. I suppose I was an outsider to the system, not held to any job description.

Once in the deputy warden's office, I said to him, "Mike, you are going to have to tell your story."

By this time, his parole officer, Richard, had been called – and a few other staff.

He told his story to the warden – everything. And after that they went to the shop right away. They searched the place and found everything exactly where he said it would be.

The next day we had another meeting.

The same people were in the office to discuss what to do with Mike. They asked the psychiatrist, "What do you think?"

He said without any hesitation, "I think he should be sent to the SHU. We never know what he is going to do."

I addressed the psychiatrist first. "With all due respect, sir, I think you want him to go to the SHU just to cover your ass."

Just like that. Actually, I think that is why they appreciated me.

I was straight with them.

And then I said, "What do you think you are doing? Sending that kid to the SHU in his state of mind is sending him to his death. His plan to escape was suicidal and he knew it. He said as much. We cannot send a 17-year-old kid to any SHU in this country. I am OK if we send him to a maximum institution, but not the SHU."

I still believe in my heart that this kid needed nurturing, not torturing.

Then the deputy warden said, "Rene, you are right. We will not send him to the SHU" The warden nodded, "I agree with that also. We are going to keep him locked in the back."

He was supposed to be sent to Edmonton max but since it was full, they created a maximum unit in the back of Stony. They called it Unit Five.

I was happy with that, then I called the drug officer, Jerry.

I said, "Jerry, you have to work with this kid."

I found it helped to put a young inmate together with the program director. Jerry was a great program officer for drugs. He had worked with the worst drug offender you can have in the system. And Jerry was able to help this guy change – his approach was different, and Jerry had helped them to see that the drugs were not good for themselves.

And Jerry knew Michael, because he had worked with him. I said, "You, do something and work with him."

Then I sat down with his parole officer.

I said, "We are going to bounce him from me, to you and to Jerry." One day it was Jerry, one day it was his parole officer, and one day it was me. We would just go over to Unit Five, and sit down with him, and talk, and together to try and help him.

About a year later, I went to see the deputy warden, and I said, "I got a problem. This Michael kid should not be in isolation – Unit Five – for more than one year. He has been doing very well over the last year."

The deputy warden said, "You know, you are right. We are going to put him back into the population."

Small improvements like that slowly built my credibility among staff.

The more successful I was with the inmates, the more I could do for them.

The more I can do, the more I want to do.

Another incident occurred in Stony. The offender was Jack. And I knew Jack from doing time with him. I knew how crazy he was.

It was on the second floor. Jack had broken a broom handle and was wielding it like a knife.

He was threatening Steve, who was a program officer working next door to my office.

Jack was angry and wanted to stab Steve. I went upstairs, and jumped in front of Jack and said, "Jack, you will not fuckin' do that. You will not do that; you have to go through me. You cannot start doing this. You are going to die in jail, and you are going to go die in the SHU because they will never tolerate this, and you are already on a really short string here." He had already killed two people with an axe. He was a real sick puppy.

He had also harmed people in prison with a knife.

I stopped him, he stopped right there. He gave me the stick, and I said, "Are you coming with me?"

I walked him right to Unit Five in the back, and they locked him up, and I said, "I will see you in a day or so."

These guys that knew me, trusted me, and respected me. I told them all the time, "I will never lie for you, because if I lie for you, I will screw up my ability to help hundreds of my other clients. Don't expect to gain my favor for nothing. If you cross me, I will be the worst guy you can meet on the planet. But if you do what you are supposed to do, I will be the guy who will advocate for you, plead your cause, and represent your case in a way that will get you what you deserve to get."

Chapter Fourteen
Redemption

Almost immediately on my release from Stony Mountain, I started telling my story. I found out that people wanted to hear my story - especially young people. Schools were asking me to speak.

I had a story that kept their attention — and I used it to warn them and everyone about the cost of breaking the law. I wanted to pay back my debt to society. You can use the term payback, but for me it was like owing and never paying back. Because I did so much bad, how can you use timeframe to pay back?

I don't know if I can use the rewards payback. It is crazy to put it this way, it is not payback it is owing. You always feel you owe something you never pay back. For me it was never enough.

They would have called me for ten schools in the week, and I would have gone to ten schools. I actually lost track of the count. I don't know how many conferences in schools and they were all different....

Even The United Way were calling me sometimes up to five speaking engagements on the same day, and I said yes.

And they would write me.

One student wrote, "I learned that the first stolen chocolate bar is going to affect the rest of your life."

Another student wrote, "I found it easier to hear from him not to break the law than from a teacher because he had already committed several crimes and spent time in jail…. I also learned that when Mr. Durocher stole money from the armored truck, he still wasn't happy with being a millionaire. My point is that stealing something because you want it doesn't make you feel good when you get it without earning it yourself."

Letters from the teachers. "We feel there is a desperate need for more frank and open discussions on topics such as crimes, consequences, incarceration and their effects on the person involved and their families. If more young people were exposed to this type of learning experience, there most certainly would be an effect on crime rates."

When I read these letters. I felt better about myself.

Then in 1992, I was a guest speaker at Kelvin High School.

I was to speak at about 10:30 a.m.

When I got there, the person taking care of the program said to me, "Hey, Rene, you are early."

I have been early for everything in my life. I panic if I am going to be late. I cannot be late for anything; I don't know why. I guess it's the way I've lived my life. My life was always

"You cannot be late" because you are going to miss something important, and for me it was, part of my life for everything that I was doing.

The woman said, "You know, Rene, there is a woman I would like you to meet. She is also speaking and I would like you to come and listen to her."

I sat down, and heard Wilma Derksen's story for the first time. I was touched. I felt, "I am lucky I didn't kill anybody."

Then I realized that it wasn't for lack of trying.

As soon as Wilma Derksen finished speaking, the woman said, "Come and I'll introduce you to Wilma."

When we met her, she told Wilma who I was and asked if Wilma could stay. Wilma said, "Yes, I will be able to stay but please don't be offended if I get up halfway through, because I have an appointment."

I said, "No worries. Do whatever you need to do."

I don't know if Wilma had heard about me before, but I think that my story was having an impact on all the students and teachers, and even on Wilma, that day.

Whenever I told my story, I always tried 100% to never glamorize crime, to never glamorize the fact that I had stolen $2,000,000. Whether I had stolen $2,000,000 or two dollars, both are crimes. The only difference is the amount of money. The harm, the hurt, the fear are all the same – only the amount of money changes.

Crime is often glorified. It is false to present someone who has stolen a big chunk of money as a hero. I was careful to make sure the kids did not glorify the life of crime.

I even told my stories on the radio. During this time, I also received a call from Peter Warren, talk radio host for CJOB, known as a top Canadian investigative journalist.

He wanted me to appear on his program. I wasn't one of his regular listeners, and he wasn't my favorite. He was a bit tough – too judgmental and punishment-oriented for me. His philosophy – "lock them up and throw away the key" – was too extreme for my liking. He was a pretty hard-ass kind of guy.

But I have to give respect to people like Warren. He wasn't afraid to challenge his audience, and if he started to believe in you, you were having a pretty good conversation with him. He was not trying to destroy his guests, he was just trying to show people that a person like me, a criminal, could be human. He never gave up. He always went on and on.

I won't forget the first time I accepted his invitation – and he challenged me. I remember him saying… "You know, Rene, what made me a believer in you and rehabilitation of criminals is the answer you gave to that young kid. You could have played the star and given an autograph."

At one of the schools where I spoke, a kid asked me for my autograph. I refused and told him, "You ask people like Wayne Gretzky for their autographs, not a guy like me." Warren said, "You could have destroyed his values – led him astray, but you didn't, and this is what made me a believer in you."

Peter Warren said that is what made him believe in me. He was a tough man.

Then talk show host Richard Cloutier had asked me to be on his afternoon show. I was almost late. I was never late.

He was wondering where I was.

"What happened to you?" he asked.

"I rolled my car – grabbed a taxi – and I am here." I told him. "It landed on the roof and I got out through the front window. The ambulance was there in five minutes. They wanted to take me to the hospital. But I said I have an appointment. I need a cab. The ambulance phoned for a cab and here I am."

Richard appeared alarmed.

He wondered if I should do this....

"I'm okay," I said.

I was superman in jail and out of jail.

Then things changed for me again. Tom French passed away four years later so I became the leader of Life Line program across the country.

I was going around training guys at the same time I was doing my job at Stony.

I was part of the taskforce that wrote the report on long-term offenders currently serving time under the supervision of CSC.

I was now working and visiting with: Ken Peterson, Warden, Mission Institution (Pacific Region), Correctional Service of Canada; Linda McLaren, Director, Program Development and Implementation, Correctional Service of Canada; Jim Murphy, Project Manager, Community Corrections, Correctional Service of Canada; Simonne

Ferguson, Regional Director (Ontario Region), National Parole Board;Yvon Lacombe, Project Manager, Regional Headquarters, (Quebec Region), Correctional Service of Canada; Lou Drouillard, Community Representative, Windsor; Ole Ingstrup, Commissioner, Correctional Service of Canada; Lucie McClung, Senior Deputy Commissioner, Correctional Service of Canada; Brendan Reynolds, Deputy Commissioner, Ontario Region, Correctional Service of Canada; Willie Gibbs, Chairman, National Parole Board; Edward Graham, Executive Director, St. Leonard's House, Windsor; John Braithwaite, Life Line National Resource Group; Wilton Goodstriker, Correctional Service of Canada Aboriginal Advisory Committee; Nancy Stableforth, Deputy Commissioner for Women, Correctional Service of Canada.

We were working on structuring the program.

The job description of the In-Reach worker was challenging.

Here it is:

The In-Reach worker must assess and understand the needs of lifers and long-term offenders during the incarceration and community phases of their sentences. They will also provide those inmates with ongoing support and advice that will enable them to adjust to the daily reality of institutional life and acceptance of their sentence.

The In-Reach workers actively encourage individual lifers to contribute to the management of their own sentences by informing them of the programs available, the case management process and other appropriate resources in institutions and in the community. In-Reach workers participate as well in Parole hearings and Judicial Reviews and assist lifers and long-term offenders in dealing with decisions of such hearings.

In-Reach Workers were peers with lived experience who assisted Lifers adapt to life within the correctional environment, and encouraged the constructive use of time while in the institution

The job description was stiff and challenging.

I was working on all of this with great, well-known people -- national leaders who taught me so much. I was on a steep learning curve. They became my mentors.

But I think I taught them as well.

If there was a specific item that I was concerned about, these guys always supported me.

They wanted to start an In-Reach worker at $20,000 salary.

The first thing I said to them. "Some of them were already earning $20,000 at other places. The temptation would be so great to do something wrong." And then I said, "…the only way to keep the safety is to make a minimum of $32,000 a year, plus $12,000 expenses."

How can you make someone live on $20,000 a year, when he has come out of prison five years before and is trying to succeed? It is like to send him back in the prison because he is going to fail, he is going to bring the stuff in jail, or whatever that is?

They all agreed that it was reasonable.

For me they were my two greatest concerns, the wage and our autonomy in the prisons. I wanted all the other workers to have the same access and freedom in prison that I had.

But it was not possible, because it was at the discretion of each warden, and some wardens were still from the Stone Age, and they didn't want having an ex-con loose in the prison. Me I was loose in Stony. I could just tell the staff, I need to see someone and they would open the door."

I was getting the door opened like I was a staff assistant.

Sometimes as a joke they would ask, "Are you the warden here?"

"No, but close to."

They knew the warden trusted me so they let me do my work. It was amazing.

But I didn't care about that. For me it was, "Let's accomplish what we need to do."

But to do this work they have to give you the tools to do the job. In Stony, I was no different than any staff.

Another thing – these Lifers were in jail for a long time. My good friend, Jim Murphy, he was a Project Officer in Community Operations in Ottawa, would ask, "What does that do to relationships that you once had on the outside … they disappear. Your relationships need to be developed on the inside. Can they be maintained for years and years?"

Lifers had to learn to live with the same group for years – isolated. They needed to develop peer support.

We started a Lifers' peer support group. We set up a lounge for them – it was a good program.

Yes, I was lucky to be involved with Life Line. It is a... my greatest asset regarding work, my work in prison is Life Line. Without Life Line I would not be here, I would not be writing this book.

Life Line was even recognized by the American Correction Association, as one of the ten biggest programs in the world. It is how it was Life Line. In August 1998, Life Line was recognized as a "best practice" by the American Correctional Association.

CHAPTER FIFTEEN
Lifers' Lounge

But I had another challenge. Wilma asked me if she could talk to me. We met for breakfast at the Original Pancake House, that is now Earls, at Polo Park. I was a bit leery of meeting with her because I didn't know how she would react to someone like me. No one had given me an idea of what she was like. This was 1992 and her daughter had been murdered in 1984. Eight years is not long in the life of a victim. I was very nervous and I think that she was too.

Wilma wanted to understand offenders so she would call me once in a while. I never called her.

It's as if Wilma was researching me to see who I really was, and I was trying to figure out how to talk to her. I didn't want to say something that would set her back three or four years. I was very careful when I was talking to her. I didn't want to harm her. She had already been harmed. I had never dealt with a victim in my life.

I was still in the process of wondering who this Wilma Derksen was. I was always reticent to ask her questions.

I was afraid of her, if I can use that term. I felt so out of place. You look at a mother with that kind of story and you look at a guy like me with my kind of story, and then you understand why it was not comfortable for me as a person to approach someone like her.

I didn't feel that it was my place. I didn't know how to take her. I respected her but I didn't know what was inside her heart. I was afraid to ask her questions. I didn't feel it was right for a guy like me to do that. I was on the defensive. I didn't want to push the questions too far. I didn't want to intrude in her life. Since I didn't want to ask her directly, I looked for other ways to get to know her.

When I met with others, I asked them about her. I think I respected Wilma more than I feared her. I respected that she was a victim and, as a criminal, I felt that I couldn't grill her. Wilma had the upper hand. I felt that if Wilma had something to tell me, she would – or somebody else would.

I didn't mind what questions Wilma asked. Nothing was out of bounds. I was an open book. That's how I lived my life. When I worked in Stony, I tiptoed around - walked on eggshells.

In prison if you make one mistake, you are done. Either you are on the side of the staff or you are on the side of the offender. If you lose one of these sides, you may as well pack up your things. I knew how to walk the fine line. I have walked a fine line all my life. I knew I would walk a fine line at Stony and also the fine line of victims.

It was like I was beginning my life. I didn't know how to approach a victim of an offender homicide. I didn't know what to say. I was in a panic. I didn't want to say something that would offend Wilma. Even one simple word might offend her.

When we met, sometimes Wilma had a high day or a low day or sometimes she seemed angry. She was like a volcano – all emotion – ready to blow. I never knew how to take her. I became more afraid. I had never met a victim in my life before – although I had created more victims that I can count. I was walking in an unfamiliar world but it was a challenge for me.

Wilma continued to be a challenge for me – an enigma. Wilma was soft-spoken – with a velvet glove and a hand of steel. I felt that she might explode if someone made the wrong approach toward her. People didn't give me that kind of information.

Wilma asked me, "What makes you tick? Will you ever rob a bank again? Will you ever be a criminal again?" I answered, "No, I can only promise you what I will do today." I think that I was being honest with Wilma and she started to develop a trust in me. It's just what I felt.

Graham was with John Howard and he knew her a little bit. I also found out about her through the media. Every time I turned around it seemed they were talking about Wilma Derksen.

But slowly we talked. She was a journalist and asked me questions.

Then the breakthrough came when we presented together. I'm not sure exactly how it happened. I think it was in 1994 in Winnipeg at a hotel near the airport, I don't remember the name of the hotel. I just remember that the John Howard Society had organized a presentation for the restorative justice community, and we were asked to be joint guest speakers. It was the first time that they put us in a dialogue together to show a victim presentation and offender presentation together.

From there on in, we did quite a bit of work together. Even though we were from opposite points of view and totally different experiences, hers was murder, mine robbery, we represented the extremes of both crimes.

Even though I had never killed anyone, I was an offender. For me a crime is a crime. I never believed my crime was better or worse than someone who had killed, or raped or whatever. The actual cost, life, money or trauma isn't different. The hostile gesture of putting the gun to someone and threatening, "Give me the money or I will kill you," is as traumatic as someone witnessing a killing. Threatening murder is equal to murder.

The more I worked with lifers at Stony, the more I asked them, "What do you want in life?" They had to understand one very important thing – I would never lie on their behalf. I told them that all the time. "If I lie for you, my other client will pay the price- and I will lose my credibility."

I was just getting to know them. It was necessary to meet with them a few times and dig and dig. They are like onions that have to be peeled and peeled because there is so much hiding inside. I had a knack for getting the guys to talk to me. I told them, "If you think I am going to lie for you, you're dreaming. If you are going to lie to me, then find somebody else to work with you.

"You have the right to work with me, but I also have the right to not work with you." I always told them that it is a two-way street. "If you want to work with me, we will sit down and have a discussion. Then we will set up a plan for you and look at what you have to do." I was pushy with the staff.

In the same way as I was teaching my clients not to lie, I didn't want to lie to Wilma either during our meetings.

I had started to work at Stony, and I was dealing with my lifers.

At one of our meetings, I asked Wilma if she had ever visited other inmates, she said yes but she had always been with other victims like her.

Then I told her that she needed to go to prison and talk to lifers just by herself.

I said, "You are asking me questions I cannot answer. I need to introduce you to people who have taken lives, so that you can talk to them directly." I was able to arrange a meeting.

I went to the warden, Art Makujt for permission.

In preparing for this meeting, I had told him, "I don't want anybody there. These guys will not open up if there is other staff present. They will open up with me, when Wilma is there, as long as there is no other staff."

The guys were always afraid to have staff there because they would put something about what had been said in their file. I said to the warden, "You know the way I am. Nobody will be harmed. I handpicked these guys." Some of these guys were badasses, but I knew all the other guys I had hand-selected would not be disrespectful toward Wilma.

They had respect for people. I didn't want to have a loose cannon in there because I didn't know how the evening would go.

I had made them aware that Wilma might ask any kind of question.

I was on one side of the room and Wilma was across from me, with the lifers all around.

When Wilma was sitting there, I could see that she was not the bravest person on the planet.

It was the first time that Stony had left me on my own with the lifers. I was fortunate that they allowed me to be by myself with an outside guest, and no other staff.

That night there were ten guys. I told Wilma, "There is only one rule. You can ask any question you want from any one of the guys."

Wilma asked them questions. "Who are you?" "Why did you kill?" "Who did you kill?" "Why?" "How do you feel now?"

All the guys were afraid because they had come face-to-face with their crime for the first time in their life. It was important for me the way the evening went. I gained insight into the guys. Wilma was there with her journalist hat, asking questions, rather than as a mother/victim. She wasn't mad at them. Both the journalist and the mother/victim wanted to know why they had committed murder.

Wilma, as a reporter, asked the right questions. I had told the guys prior to the meeting, "Wilma has the right to ask any question at all. If some of you can't take it, leave and don't come to the meeting." No one left.

As Wilma asked her questions, I was looking ahead to the next person in the circle whose turn was coming.

I trusted what the guys were saying when they spoke to Wilma. They couldn't lie because this was the first time they were face-to-face with a family victim of homicide. They were petrified. I felt that right away. When I sit with lifers, I feel everything that they are feeling. It's as if it's in my bones. I knew it myself – if you expect to change your life, you are going to have to face your worst demons.

I could see the guys were afraid of what question Wilma might ask him. His face was white and pale. These guys didn't know Wilma either. They didn't know if she was looking for revenge or answers.

When Wilma got to Driskell, he said, "I am the odd ball at this meeting. I am not guilty. I didn't kill anybody. I never killed that guy." I was surprised at his answer and I didn't want him to explain any further which might have sounded like a denial, so I just said, "OK. Next."

Then later I said, "Come in my office," and I asked him all that stuff.

This was the first time that I had heard Driskell say, "I didn't kill anybody." When I had met with him before, he told me, "I'm not guilty." But every guy in jail says he's not guilty.

But when he said that to Wilma, I was convinced. After that, I went to see him and we spoke privately. I said, "Tell me your story." I believed him and he was the first one we took for the Association for the Defense of the Wrongly Convicted.

It was quite an evening for me. I felt, "Oh my god, we can do something in this place." Everyone told me that the lifers were a waste of time. Every few months the lifers' room would be closed because they found a shank or another weapon there.

My relationship with Wilma became closer than I had expected. The interactions with the ten lifers helped Wilma, as well as helping the lifers. The lifers were terrified of Wilma.

They didn't know how Wilma would react, what she would say. These guys knew what they would say. They wanted to tell their stories but they had no idea about Wilma's story. After meeting Wilma, and seeing her respond in these situations, my trust in victims grew and I was prepared to do another meeting with other victims.

After the lifers had met with Wilma, I was able to get the lifers' room opened in the daytime. I told the guys, "If you lose this privilege, you are the owner of that. You guys have to search the room yourselves – every night. I don't want to know what you find but, but if you don't empty the room of all the crap in there, they will shut it down. A time will come when I won't be able to reopen it." I had already reopened it many times.

The guys knew they had to police themselves and that's what they did. If they found weapons, they would throw them in the garbage. They didn't want to lose their room. It became quite important because I started having social activities with the lifers' families.

Two years after this meeting – which changed both of us -- I invited Wilma to come and speak at the Lifers Awareness Day '99 at Stony Mountain Institution, in another part of the complex, another gymnasium. I had invited community offender agencies to present their programs, much like a trade show.

She told her story this time.

Everyone was impressed with her.

After she left, the guys and I were talking.

"You guys always tell me that you want to do something. Why don't you put your money where your mouth is?"

"What do you want us to do?"

"Think about it. Maybe we can do something great here."

One guy said, "Why can't we raise money?"

"Now, we're talking."

There were lots of ideas on the table.

I said, "What about a Candace Derksen Fund?"

It wasn't much but we tried.

Because I was receiving money for speaking in the community, I would donate it all to the fund held in The Winnipeg Foundation. I spoke to over a hundred schools, received over 520 letters from students. And kept them all.

Though I never felt it was enough.

I owed.

Around that time, I had gone to speak with another victims' group in the city. I didn't know anything about that group. I had never met anyone and I didn't know anyone there. Their president had called me a few times and had called me about the paper…you know I was starting to get published all over the place.

When they asked me to speak, I said, "No problem," but I didn't know what I was walking into. They were really explosive

I told my story and talked about what I was trying to do. The president wanted to get involved with me, but then I found out that they were very volatile. Lots of them were not ready to be involved in a situation like Wilma's.

They were still so angry, and with anger on both sides, you cannot solve anything.

There was one more thing that came out of that Lifers' Lounge meeting.

At the Stony Mountain meeting with Wilma Derksen and the ten lifers, it was Jim Driskell who had said, "I'm the oddball here. I'm not guilty."

He had been convicted in 1991 in the death of Perry Dean Harder.

It was because of him that I became a founding board member of the Association in the Defence of the Wrongly Convicted in Manitoba.

It was this Association that eventually took up the case and challenged key evidence used to put Driskell behind bars.

After spending 13 years in prison for a murder he didn't commit, Driskell was offered $4,000,000 in compensation from the province and city. The Crown had accused Driskell of killing Harder in the back of his van, pointing to three hairs in the van that an RCMP lab labelled as belonging to Harder.

However, DNA tests done in England at the request of the Association later revealed none of the hairs belonged to Harder.

Driskell was released on bail in 2003 and the Federal Justice Minister quashed the conviction in 2005. The Crown didn't pursue another trial.

CHAPTER SIXTEEN
Toilet Paper

Because of these encounters, both Wilma and I believed that we could help other crime victims. That is when I started to believe in face-to-face programs. That is the best thing that can happen to anyone. A victim and offender. If the victims are given the right to see what they want, and have the offender there, and are willing to take whatever they have been told, then that's what matters to me.

The guys would tell me their stories. In a population of 120 or 130 lifers in Stony and Rockwood, you will never have everyone working with you. Some of the guys were still at the point in their lives where they just wanted to try to give you their sob story. There was nothing there, and I kicked some of them out of the program when I was doing time. I was not shy about kicking someone out.

I always told my clients, "You can never give me a sob story – 'Poor me, poor me.' You can't. I don't care what led up to the point where you killed the person. I don't care what led you to cross that line. I was just lucky."

It seemed as if Wilma's presence was important as somebody who raised questions. If Wilma hadn't been there, the lifers wouldn't have come and, if they had come, they would never have told their stories. Wilma was the safeguard that the lifers needed. I was the most rigid person that they had, because I knew all about the manipulation, the lying and the bullshit. Walk the walk, and talk the talk.

She asked them questions that they had to answer – questions that no one had asked them before. "Who are you? What made you do that?" Wilma didn't ask the questions in anger. She just said, "I want to know."

The questions opened them up – like peeling back the layers of an onion. No one in the group had ever faced a victim before. It was an emotional wake-up call for them.

This is the reason why I was opposed to the way Stony was working. They wanted me to take offenders into the program late in their sentence. I said, "No. The earlier we can get them into the program, the better it is going to be for them, because they will start to peel the onion sooner. It could take years." But if they don't start to open up and talk about what they did and why they did it, they won't find answers and how can you get them released eventually?

At the second meeting Lynne L`Heureux Hoger came in and told her story.

She knew me from before. We had a meeting at one of my presentations. In my presentation, I said that I had married a girl from St. Pierre and that I had hurt her. I didn't know that there was anyone there from St. Pierre. Later Lynne asked, "Is your wife Suzanne? I grew up next door to her in St. Pierre."

Lynne said, "I know Suzanne. We grew up together."

I thought, "I am going to get it now," but Lynne said, "I hated you before you came to talk to us, but now after I have heard you speak, I don't." Then I learned the whole story. Suzanne and her sister and Lynne had hung around together when they were younger

Meanwhile Lynne's brother had been killed and felt she needed to speak to a lifer so we set up another meeting in prison with Wilma, another woman who had lost her daughter, I forget her name, and Lynne. The lifers were Dennis, Jerry, Mike, and the last one was an adopted kid, Cameron, who had killed his friend in Calgary with a construction gun.

There were three victims and four lifers.

I was really impacted by this meeting. At the beginning, Lynne and the other woman didn't want to shake hands with the lifers. I said to them, "Do whatever you want and don't do anything you don't want to do." For me, it was the best thing that could happen to my lifers. They had to meet face-to-face with what they did. This session was quite emotional. Lynne was mad when she told her story.

They were all angry. Mike was 16 when he came to Stony. He had stabbed his best friend at the school he went to.

Dennis was the first lifer to tell his story. He had killed his girlfriend, and was quite emotional. Then Cameron told his story. He also became quite emotional. Someone asked for Kleenex. We didn't have a box of Kleenex – I didn't even know such a thing existed at the time – but we had toilet paper. The toilet paper was on the side where the women were sitting because they had been telling their stories. When one of the guys started to cry, one of the women took the roll of toilet paper and rolled it across the table in his direction.

That was the most important gesture that I have ever witnessed in working with victims. She felt compassion towards that guy. It showed me that two human beings, both angry as hell – one whose anger erupted to the point of killing another person....

Anger is anger, it is just to not cross the line, and these guys did cross the line, and just to make sure that they are not able of crossing the line, she rolled the toilet paper, because this guy was so emotional that he was crying.

When I saw that gesture, I said, "Oh my god," and I still talk about it. It is the most important gesture I have ever seen. The meeting went extremely well and, at the end, the women were hugging the guys. It was amazing, because when they walked in, they didn't want to touch the guys. They wanted to sit across the table from them. I tried to reassure them by saying, "Whatever you want – just tell me. I will set up everything the way you want it. These guys are willing to take whatever you have."

I thought I was handling victimization very well – and then I met my own victim – someone I had victimized a long time ago.

It was when I was in prison and I had 28 years left to serve. I was desperate to get out. I said to myself, "I am finished in Quebec. I have to get the hell out of Quebec. What am I going to do?"

Then I talked with my partner, and I talked with my two friends in prison and started planning an escape.

I said, "Why don't we take the cultural center?" The way it was set up, we had a good place to hide without the risk of being shot, because there was only one door. We could put the big stuff in front of the door, and we could hide there, behind the stuff, with the two staff hostages.

The next day I spoke to my buddies. I said, "Listen, I don't want you to put your lives at risk because of me."

They said, "Rene, you are our partner. We don't give a fuck. We are going to do it."

"Here is what we are going to do to get out of here."

"What?"

"We are going to kidnap them. Then we will make an exchange with the administration. They ship us out of here, or we kill them."

They agreed, "OK."

I walked into the office with a shank. They all came with their shanks.

We walked up to the two staff members, Joe and Guy. I grabbed them and said, "You guys sit down. I don't want to harm you but I am going to tie you up. You don't have a choice. You have to do what I tell you, because I am going to kill you if you don't."

Joe was a great guy, a good man. I liked working with Joe. I used to say to him, "Hey, old man, let's do something today." He was probably in his mid-50s at that time. Guy was a guard. I didn't meet him until he came to work at the cultural center, during the summer holiday program. He liked doing that kind of job. Every night, every day of the week, whenever there was an activity, he was always the assigned staff.

I put the knife to Joe's throat and said, "Shut up and do as we say, because you are going to die. I don't want to hurt you."

These guys were petrified. I locked the doors of the office. I was the only one with a key. And we took cover in case they decided to shoot.

But when I took him hostage, he had to do what I said. There was no more relationship between me and him. It was my other personality that was inside. It is almost as if I had a split personality. Nothing could have stopped me. I would have killed anyone, because I wanted to go.

The negotiations started and didn't take long. I think the same day, late at night, they agreed to ship us out.

First, all four of us were locked up in the hole in Archambault.

There was a biker in the hole at the same time who I despised. Later the guards said they didn't know he was my enemy – but they knew. When they wanted a guy to settle down their problem, they did that. They let me out into the yard first. I was in the corner.

Then they threw him in. They shut the door and locked it.

He could not see me right away.

The first knock I gave him – a fist to the face – he went down. A knockout. But I kept on kicking him until they opened the door.

They pretended they didn't know and I never said a word. It was never reported.

I fuckin' beat the shit out of him. I wanted to kill him more than anything.

I wanted to kill someone. I didn't want to live anymore.

Despair, anger, powerlessness, grief did that to me.

That is when me and Gilles were shipped to Dorchester. Gaetan was shipped to Stony Mountain, and my other buddy, Bull, hanged himself in the cell. This was the worst shock for me, that this guy hanged himself. I lost a very good friend. He was not able to take it. This made me very angry.

I never gave it much thought… what my threats did to those I took hostage.

But I came face to face with it when I attended the 2001 Congress of Criminal Justice in Halifax.

Suzanne and I were in a good space so we decided to make a holiday out of it – and enjoy ourselves. We landed in Halifax.

And then I met Guy in the foyer of the hotel.

I was so stunned to see him.

I didn't know what to say to him. We tried to make amends but it was awkward. It took me a whole night to think it through. I wanted to talk to him again but there was no time.

I felt as if I had been knocked out.

The first thing the next morning, I had to tell my story on stage to the wider assembly.

I moved to the podium. I couldn't think of anything! Guy was sitting there.

I started to tell everyone. "It was back in 1975 – about 26 years ago. I was in prison. I had 28 years left to serve. I was desperate to get out. I took two men hostage…. And one is here in the audience today."

I stepped down from the podium. Guy stood up in the front row, and we embraced.

I returned to the podium and apologized publicly for what I had done – apologized again to Guy – and honored him in a beautiful way.

But after the conference, I could not let it rest. Guy had confessed to me, "Every day when I walk into the prison, I am afraid somebody is going to take me hostage again."

He was just beginning his career when I did that to him and 26 years later, he was still working in prison in Quebec – and still afraid of what could happen to him.

As a Life Line worker for CSC with connections, I started to use my influence and advocated for Guy. Two months later he received a job offer to move to Ottawa and work in the Restorative Justice Unit – a safe place.

It takes away some of the pain you have inflicted when you are able to help.

CHAPTER SEVENTEEN
Father Figure
2007

As I was trying to change, there always seemed to be two sides – law-abiding and the other. Never accepted by the law-abiding. I was on the other.

As much as I tried, I never felt accepted by the law-abiding until Washington. It was in Washington, 1998, that I moved to the other side -- figuratively and literally.

I am talking about the American Correction Association conference in the States that took place in 1998 or 1999. John was invited every year, because he had been past president.

John Braithwaite had an unforgettable impact on my life. I can't forget how important this man has been to me – like a father figure.

I will always remember my own father and what I thought….I always told myself that I would never be like him. I always saw the bad part of my father – never the good part. I am sure he had a good part... but I never saw it. I just was filled with hate – and this deep void for a father figure.

All I could think of was beating the shit out of my father – for letting me down – moving out of my life – never giving me any father model to live by – no support. I truly disowned him.

Here was another father. He impacted my life in every way, shape and form. He knew that I was doing everything to facilitate the life of my clients and he knew that I was passionate about Life Line. Every time I met John, I felt, "Oh my god, I am going to meet John again!"

John was part of the Canada Criminal Justice Association and he is the only Canadian who was president of the American Correction Association. They voted for a Canadian! Can you imagine that? I can't believe how the people in the States respected him.

He was like a god within the American Correction Association. He helped them found the ACJA and even became the first president. They had so much respect for John. It only emphasized the respect I already had for him. John Braithwaite – the man who opened every door in the States for Life Line – our light – to the Criminal Justice System.

John invited me to come with him to this conference. That visit opened everything in my life for me because I was approved to go to the States. They gave me a waiver. I applied for a waiver and I was approved.

That was when I realized I had passed over to the other side. I was associated with John – and hung out with him.

Then there was a moment when it came together.

We were to go to Maryland – which is the state right next to Washington, D.C. – just on the other side of the highway.

We wanted to cross the highway but there were so many lanes of traffic and fences. My colleague Skip had to be in Maryland at the hotel and we could have made it if we had gotten the tram. But we had gone the wrong way to get out of the hotel. We had just wanted to walk to go to the train. It wasn't even that far. But because we had made that wrong turn, it became that far and we had to jump fences or we wouldn't have made it on time otherwise.

We were walking and I think that John realized we had to climb. So he just decided to climb a seven-foot high fence. At the time he was 75 years old and jumping fences like a kid! Would I be able to do it at 60-something? Skip and I couldn't let him go by himself so we climbed the fences with him. Poor Skip was not an athlete….

I remember being shocked with what we were doing. I remember even yelling – above the traffic noise, "Where the hell did you take us, John?"

I'm going to do this too. We could have all gotten killed. It is funny. Here we are – adults involved in a program – climbing fences to get to the other side of the highway. We had to scale two or three fences. Some of them were lower, but the first one was so high. John was laughing. But we made it!

John, Skip and I were invited to the Marriott Hotel in Maryland for lunch. I had never seen a hotel like this before – nor such a lunch! I couldn't believe the food I was seeing in front of me. It was humungous. I had never seen anything like that before, because I was poor. Here I was – arriving in the capital city of the U.S.A. -- staying with this amazing man who was human but also a saint. And he was wise. I had access to all this.

Then I wandered around by myself as well… free.

I said to Skip and John, "Tomorrow I am going to take the subway," and I took the subway to Washington. I got out at the bridge by the University. I crossed the bridge on foot. There was a guy sitting on the bridge with a can for money, and there was another guy there as well. I thought to myself, "If I give money to every guy, my pockets will be empty by the time I get across the bridge."

At the time I didn't realize that this is how things were in Washington, D.C. I walked a little bit further and ended up at the Vietnam Veterans Memorial. I was not impressed with the Wall, because it was just a wall with names on it. Then I walked into a field that represented the Korean War in the 1950s. There I was impressed. There were soldiers in the field. They were not alive but the way they were arranged, they looked as if they were alive and fighting in the field. It was amazing.

I don't know how they were able to make the two fields, arrange the soldiers in line, and make it all look so realistic. I always tell anyone who is going to Washington to visit those two places. Even if they can't visit anything else, I tell them to go visit the memorials.

I did not visit all the museums, because I would still be there. Washington is such a beautiful city.

The entire time I was exploring the museums walking the streets of Washington, I had this feeling of unreality. I was on top of the world – the most powerful city in the world… and I was free.

It was John – John Braithwaite was my mentor. He is like a dad to me. He's still alive. He turned 89 on March 5, 2019. I always call him on his birthday. This year I phoned him around February 20, before I left for Cuba, to tell him I wouldn't be able to talk to him on March 5.

He's the dad I never had. I used to phone him and say, "Hey dad, how come you are taking my brother and sister on a trip, and you're not taking me?" He would laugh, because he was always taking his children on trips. This man was good to me. Everything I was able to do with Life Line and outside Life Line had his mark on it. He came to love me.

At first, he didn't want me to be part of Life Line because I was not a lifer, but he ended up loving me like a father. He still does. I call him every opportunity I get and I never miss his birthday. I never miss. It warms his heart when I call him dad.

Every time I see him, I say, "Do you remember Washington?" and we start to laugh.

There were others who had an impact on my life, but not like John.

What do they say? It takes a village to raise a child? I say, it takes a village to change a man.

It was in Washington that I realized that I had truly changed from the inside out.

But I had worked hard for that moment.

Another father figure I remember was Pierre Allard.

Archambault Penitentiary is where I got to know Pierre Allard.

I was a member of the summer holiday committee and responsible for organizing shows and activities for the two weeks – singers and guests were invited from outside.

The organizational meetings took place in the chapel.

One day Pierre Allard walked in.

I said, "Who the fuck are you?"

He said, "I am Pierre Allard."

I responded, "What is Pierre Allard?"

He said, "I am the minister."

Ordinarily I would have hated him immediately. I hated anything to do with the church, but this time...... I felt something different. I looked at his face and I saw kindness.

I hadn't seen kindness for so many years. He was a man with kindness. It didn't take long. I became a kind of friend of his, but I never talked religion with him.

I didn't want to hear a word about religion, and he knew that. But I was running the summer holiday program and using his room, his chapel, his church. The Catholic chapel was in another room. There were about five or six other rooms.

He was the only one I really wanted to talk to.

After the hostage taking in Dorchester, they jumped on me and locked me up in the hole. I was locked up in that hole for a year. I had 20 minutes to take a shower. The guards were so afraid of me that they used to put handcuffs on me when I was taking my shower and lock me to the shower bar.

When I was locked up in that cell, I started to train. I jogged for four or five hours a day and did 600 or 700 push-ups and sit-ups. I was in such great shape, I never wanted to get out. I just took my shower and said, "Stick your fuckin' walk."

Then I started to read. The first book in English I ever read was almost 1,000 pages. They made a movie of it but I can't remember the name.

Pierre Allard used to come and see me once in a while. "How are you Rene?"

Our lives became very close.

It was the beginning of a friendship that lasted.

Pierre was dedicated to his calling to give spiritual support to all of those involved in prison ministries. His work as a prison chaplain had given him insights and the vision for the new field of restorative justice, which aimed to bring communities, offenders and victims to talk about the way that crime affects a community. He was good at bringing people together and having them talk. Because of this he was able to create the volunteer Christian Council for Reconciliation, and the National Association for Chaplaincy Volunteers. Pierre Allard was the president of the International Prison Chaplains' Association.

He had read reports on my work.

I was so proud of them.

"René Durocher has been an In-Reach worker since 1994, and has dealt with an average of 120 clients a year. René has been assisting his clients by motivating them to achieve the goal of turning their life around. He has attended case conferences with the purpose of 'having his clients take charge of their own lives by planning with case managers and In-Reach workers to fulfil their case plans.'

"In addition, René attended the Offender Management Review Board to support the client in the reduction of their security clearance application. By meeting with his clients an average of once a month, René became the continuous link with his clients during their incarceration period."

Yes. It was because of my work and my relationship with Pierre that I received a Pierre Allard award. And they call it the Phoenix award. And the Phoenix, we know what is it, the bird burned, went to ash and then rose again. And the fact that Pierre Allard became so close to me, became my friend, because he followed me most of his career.

The Press Release read:

"December 17, 2008 13:51 ET

Correctional Service of Canada: Former Federal Offender Receives Award

STONY MOUNTAIN, MANITOBA

Former inmate Rene Durocher was presented the Pierre Allard Award Phoenix Award by Member of Parliament Ms. Shelly Glover (Saint Boniface) on behalf of Public Safety Minister Peter Van Loan during a ceremony held within Stony Mountain Institution on December 15, 2008.

Mr. Durocher served more than 24 years as an inmate in federal penitentiaries. He eventually earned parole consideration and returned to the community approximately 17 years ago. Since that time, he has made significant and positive contributions to the community in such a way as to serve as an inspiration for others. In 1994, Mr. Durocher gained employment as an In-Reach Worker with the Life Line Program. Through Life Line, former inmates who have successfully reintegrated into the community despite serving life sentences work in institutions to develop programs for lifers; help motivate offenders while incarcerated and during reintegration; and contribute to public safety. In June of 2000, Mr. Durocher became the National Resource Coordinator for the Life Line Program.

Mr. Durocher has been a devoted advocate of crime prevention and restorative justice strategies and has served as a volunteer with the John Howard Society of Manitoba, a contributor to the National Resource Group Task Force Report on Lifers and Long-Term Offenders in Canada, a member of the Canadian and Manitoba Criminal Justice Associations and as a founding board member of the Association in the Defence of the Wrongly Accused in Manitoba. In December 2004, Mr. Durocher received the John Howard Society of Canada Humanitarian Service Award. He has made more than 500 presentations in Manitoba schools through his Accent on Youth Program, which is designed to assist youth from making decisions that could lead them to incarceration. He continues to contribute to the betterment of inmates and society through his work with the Manitoba chapter of the St. Leonard's Society as

Volunteer Coordinator at Stony Mountain Institution.

The Pierre Allard Award was established in 2006 to honour former Correctional Service of Canada Assistant Commissioner Reverend Doctor Pierre Allard and his commitment to furthering the development of the field of restorative justice and community engagement. The award is presented annually to a former federal offender who has lived as a law-abiding citizen for at least 10 years, who has been identified by the community as a person of integrity and strength, and as someone who has been identified as a model citizen who has made significant contributions to the community through their service to the public.

Correctional Services of Canada"

CHAPTER EIGHTEEN
Tough Job

Another father figure was Willie Gibbs.

I was the meanest to him….

And yet he forgave.

I was in Springhill in 1976 when I met Willie Gibbs - the warden then. He was a great man but, at that time, he was my enemy. Even though I hated him, he was good to me.

I went to work in the kitchen after that. I was the baker and, with me, they knew that there was no shit in the food. I would not tolerate anyone putting crap in the food that was fed to the staff. I looked after the food for both the inmates and the staff.

My principle was no shit in the food. I wouldn't tolerate anyone doing this under my supervision. You can put anything in a piece of cake – like garbage – and they won't know what they are eating. Some guys think that's funny but I wouldn't let it happen. I was very proud of being a good butcher – and now a good baker. They could have tried to put drugs in the food, but nobody wants to waste drugs. They want to keep them.

About a year later, Willie said, "Rene, you have done a lot of time. Would you like to go visit your family in Quebec?"

I said, "Yes, I would like to." I went out on a TA to Montreal. I took a plane, went to see a few friends, and came back on the plane with three ounces of hash. The guys inside wanted hashish so I bought three ounces in Montreal and put it in my pocket. There was no drug detection on the plane.

Walking onto the plane with the hash was like a walk in the park. When I got back, there was a little town outside Dorchester. I didn't have to be back until the next day so I was going to stay with a guy who was also out on a TA in Oxford.

As I was walking toward the house, my friend came out to meet me. We were on the sidewalk talking and a cop stopped. He asked us who we were. As soon as he asked me, I just kept on walking as if I hadn't heard him. I dropped the bag of hash down the side of my leg. There was a little bit of snow and the drugs were on the ground. I turned around and walked back towards him.

Then I said, "I am an inmate. I've got my papers to show that I am due to go back tomorrow. I stopped here to sleep."

"What is that?"

"What?"

"That bag."

"I don't know."

He went and picked up the bag. He saw right away that it was drugs but he didn't know what kind.

"I never saw it in my life. It's not mine," I said.

And then he put us in the car and he drove us back to the penitentiary. That's when Willie Gibbs got mad at me.

"I gave you a TA and you…."

"It's not me, for fuck's sake. It's not mine."

He locked me up in the hole and he came back to see me. "Listen, Rene, if you take the blame and plead guilty, you won't have to be transferred out here."

I knew the law, so I said, "OK, but on one condition – I have to be taken to court tomorrow. I plead guilty tomorrow and am sentenced tomorrow."

He called whomever he had to call. They came to pick me up and take me to court. When I went to court, I was charged with possession of illegal drugs.

Then I said, "Not guilty and I want my trial next week."

They set up the date for my trial the next week but, back then they needed 30 days to have hashish analyzed to see if it is the real thing.

When I got back to court, the judge said, "We are going to have to drop the charge because we can't get the results to see if it is real hash or not."

So I was acquitted. When I went back, Willie Gibbs said, "You are going to the max."

I replied. "You know when I get fucked, I like to get kissed at the same time."

He left me in that cell, and three days later my transfer was arranged to go back to Dorchester.

Willie Gibbs was so angry at me that he drove the van himself to take me to Dorchester. He was really angry with me, specifically because he had just given me five Unescorted Temporary Absences (UTAs)

When you were living in jail away from the other region, Quebec in my case, they gave you a day to travel one way, a day to travel the other way and three UTAs. I ended up in Dorchester.

While in Dorchester. I put in a grievance against Willie Gibbs. I didn't know if I would win the grievance or not. I said, "Ha I know I will win my grievance."

He did it the wrong way and the judge threw out the case. When I told him I would rather get kissed before I get fucked, he turned red. He was so mad at me.

Later I was told, "You know what Rene? You are going to Stony Mountain."

I said, "I thought I was going back to Springhill."

"No. You are involved in a grievance. We are sending you to another medium – Stony Mountain."

"OK." I knew that my partner was there. "OK. I will see my partner there."

He put on the handcuffs and put me on the plane. There were two guards with me. I think it was in 1979.

Later when I started working as an In-Reach worker at Stony Mountain, we worked together on the national program.

Through my work, he forgave me.

He was good to me.

Willie published a book in 2004 called, *The Cons and the Pros the Tough Job of Helping Offenders.*

This is what he wrote about me.

Then there was the case of Rene Durocher. He was definitely one of the most interesting, albeit challenging, individuals I have had the privilege to work with over the years. He was not on my caseload when he was in Springhill around 1978, as I was already warden by then. His stay was relatively brief. At the time, he was basically a hard-core hoodlum from Montreal who had somehow slipped through the cracks and been transferred to a medium-security institution when he should have been in a maximum.

He had been admitted to the old St. Vincent-de-Paul fortress for the first time in 1961, and had been in and out of penitentiaries ever since. His speciality was armed robbery. In fact, in the 1980s, several years after I had him returned to maximum security, he pulled his biggest job while on mandatory supervision – a two million-dollar robbery of a Brinks truck in Toronto. For that daring heist, he received his longest sentence: sixteen years, plus whatever was left of his un-served mandatory supervision period.

While Rene was at Springhill, we made the mistake of granting him an unescorted temporary absence. Although he returned as expected, he had found time in between to conclude a drug deal in Oxford, a small town near Springhill. The police caught up with him, but he would not admit to being involved or to bringing the drugs into the institution. Once we found proof, he was quickly transferred back to Dorchester.

I didn't hear anything from or about Rene for many years, until the autumn of 1995 when I attended the Canadian Congress of Criminal Justice in Winnipeg. It turned out that Rene was also a delegate.

He came over to re-introduce himself and to remind me, with tongue-in-cheek, of our last encounter in Springhill, about *fifteen years earlier. He was obviously very pleased and proud to have left his life of crime behind. Since his release on parole in 1991, he had been working to help his fellow cons, especially lifers and other long-term offenders. He had also built a solid family life with his wife, Suzanne, and their two children.*

One of the activities on the conference program was a visit to Stony Mountain Penitentiary, located a few kilometres outside Winnipeg. There we would learn about the Life Line program Rene directed for long-term offenders. After the visit, a group of us crowded into a van with Rene driving. He took great pleasure in reminding me, in the presence of the seven or eight others, that he and I were experiencing a dramatic reversal of roles. The last time we'd been together, I had ordered him transferred by van from a medium to a maximum-security penitentiary. It was not a particularly pleasant memory for him. He joked that now he was not only in charge of the van, but also of a mechanism that could open the back door and drop the rear (where I was sitting) onto the highway!

Life Line aims to help lifers and other long-term offenders both inside and outside correctional institutions. John Braithwaite (Life Line's president and founder), Skip Graham (Director of the St. Leonard's Society's halfway house in Windsor, Ontario), Rene, and I have, over the years, made many presentations to correctional and criminal justice conferences both nationally and internationally on the subject of Life Line.

One of our last joint presentations was at the 2001 Congress of Criminal Justice in Halifax. While he was speaking at the workshop, Rene noticed and acknowledged a man in the audience, by the name of Guy Lariviere, a former staff member of Archambault Institution in the Quebec region. While serving time in that facility many years earlier, Rene and two other inmates had taken Lariviere and another correctional employee hostage.

Guy and Rene had not seen one another in the intervening twenty-six years. On the opening day of the Conference, they spotted each other in the hotel lobby, and both remembered their last "meeting" in Archambault Institution. Somewhat strangely, but without any hesitation, they embraced and agreed to meet the following day to talk about their respective journeys since that famous encounter in 1975. During the conversation, Rene painfully acknowledged that, with all the acts of violence he had committed during his criminal life, this was the first time he could meet one of his victims in person and ask for forgiveness. Both were extremely shaken, but grateful to have had this opportunity for closure.

Back at the workshop, Rene was in a highly emotional state, and expressed his sorrow over having committed such a violent act, and his difficulty in coming face to face with Guy. Guy was extremely touched by Rene's words, and tears were rolling down his face. It was obvious he was prepared to forgive. Suddenly, Rene stepped down from the podium, Guy stood up in the front row, and the two men embraced. We were sharing one of the most spontaneous and sincere gestures of restorative justice that I had ever witnessed.

Incidentally, Guy Lariviere, being close to the end of his correctional career, is currently on a two-year secondment from the Correctional Service of Canada to the Canadian Criminal Justice Association, of which I am currently president.

The Life Line concept is based on a partnership between voluntary community agencies like the St. Leonard's Society and the Correctional Service of Canada and National Parole Board. Its mission is to provide, through in-reach workers who are all reformed lifers or long-term offenders on parole, opportunities for inmates and parolees to reform. It has been around for a little over ten years, and has been remarkably successful. Rene is now the senior in-reach worker. Aside from his regular duties in Manitoba and Stony Mountain Pen, he monitors various Life Line programs across the country and trains other in-reach workers.

Rene is now able to appreciate the harm he did during his criminal career and to empathize with victims. He has become a close friend and associate of Wilma Derksen whose daughter, Candace, was murdered in 1984. Wilma wrote a book about her tragic ordeal, Have You Seen Candace? and became not only a victims' advocate, but also a proponent of offender rehabilitation.

On February 1, 2002, Rene finally reached the warrant expiry of his sentence after more than forty years. That means he has successfully completed his parole and is a free man. I made sure to send him my sincere congratulations. 2002

p.72-75

When Willie Gibbs was dying, I got John Braithwaite to ask Willie's wife, Doreen, if I could call him. About two weeks later, the phone rang. It was Willie. "Hi, Rene. How are you? It is so good to talk to you." I said, "Oh my god, I cannot believe it." Here he was on his death bed and he took the time to pick up the phone and call me. He was barely able to talk but we had a ten-minute conversation.

I said to him, "Willie, I know I am going to follow you eventually, but I just don't know where I'm going because I'm not a good candidate for heaven. I am a good candidate for hell."

He said, "No, Rene. You did good things." We talked a bit longer and he said, "So long, my friend."

He called me his friend right up to the last minute. I was one of the last people he spoke to. It was such an honour. I was very proud of that relationship.

I still don't feel good about what I did to him way back then. I am so glad he called me a few days before he died. The fact that he took the time to call me before he died, as one of the people closest to him. The fact that he saw me as someone close to him made me better.

CHAPTER NINETEEN
Superman Surgery

Even to this day, I don't believe in man-made religion. In the Roman Catholic Church, there is always a middle man between you and God and you have to tell the man why. It was my experience that the priests just tried to attract kids and abuse them. Part of my heart hated them as much as I can hate anything in the world.

How the heck do you let a man, the person come between you and the most powerful in the history of the world, God? We were raised to fear God.

The priests were trying to control us. It was a better way to control us, and through that the politics in Quebec. The province had decided it would be good to increase the population. So the priest would come for a home visit those days… and telling father and mother, "If you don't have kids don't have sex." It was like this. It was manipulation.

When I grew up, I looked at all those stories of priests abusing other children, and I saw what some of the priests did to me so in my mind, it was all of them who did that because a kid cannot separate it out. It's all of the priests. That's the only reason I'm staying away. It's really amazing.

However, I do believe there is a God and I don't believe he needs a middle man between him and me. I strongly believe I will never have a middle man between him and me. If he is all over the place and if he is powerful like God is supposed to be, why would he need a middle man to contact him?

That's the way I look at it. I don't need anyone to be my middle man. If God can't hear me, there is a problem with him. He's got my number. He's got to have my number.

But now that I am an adult, I know that you can't tar them all with the same brush. It doesn't make sense that every priest is bad. However, that was my experience growing up and after I chose the life of crime. I never wanted to practice religion.

I did become friends with Pierre Allard. But, for me, he was not a priest but a minister. Priests are Catholic. Ministers are Protestant. Pierre never represented a priest for me. We became friends.

I talked with Pierre Allard. I said, "I want to be friends with you but I won't talk about religion. I don't believe in man-made religion." Pierre never asked what had happened to me as a youth. We were good friends and respected one another. I knew that he would respect my point of view, just as I respected his.

I don't discuss religion; I don't believe that God needs a middle man. I grew up in Quebec with the fear of God in me.

But this is the way I am. I believe in God. I don't have any doubts about that. I'd have to be crazy to not believe in God. All those years I believed I was Superman. I don't think I was Superman but there was a power that kept me alive. Why didn't I get a bullet in my head instead of my partner?

There is a power. I don't doubt that – otherwise I wouldn't believe in anything. I believe that you have to believe in something to be able to move on with your life.

I have to believe there's a power higher than me that makes things happen because I'm not Superman anymore.

I ask, "Why didn't I get the bullet? Why did my partner get two in the back and not me?" There were 72 bullet holes in the car and I didn't get hit at all. I started to question things. "My God, I wasn't that Superman after all." I was questioning things and looking for answers.

I still don't know. I don't know why I'm still alive when I was the first target up front. I was the one protecting the others in the bank. I should have been the first to be taken down when they saw the machine gun. Everyone in the car around me was injured – but I wasn't. I got out of the car and kept running until I got to the school wall. I turned the gun on myself but it jammed. Why didn't I die that day? I shouldn't have still been alive in my situation. I wanted to kill myself. But I didn't die and I didn't want to go back to jail.

I have respect for God. I didn't turn around or pray or anything. It never occurred to me to do that. Sometimes I do talk to God.

I did it way back with David when he was killed. Why him and not me? It's funny. I was willing for it to be me. Why him? I don't know.

I've asked questions but I'm always afraid of the answers. Because I've lived a life like this, I've tried to stay away from those questions. But then everything started to evolve in my life.

I said, "Oh, my God. I'm not crazy. I know there is a superpower."

My god, I shouldn't be sitting here. I used to play Russian roulette with a gun to my head when I was 16 or 17. I didn't care about life.

I discovered there is a higher power, greater than me, that makes things happen. Whatever it is, whether there is a reason or not, it is his prerogative. He has his reasons to do that and I respect that. I will never live in fear of God because I was raised to live in fear of God and I was harmed by the one who was teaching me about the fear of God. Why were they not afraid of what they were doing to kids? Why make people fear God? I am not afraid of God.

When I die, I'm not afraid to meet my creator. As a kid, I was taught to live in fear of God. When I got harmed the way I did, I started to harm others, and then I couldn't believe that I was still alive. God should have cut my life way shorter. He should have judged me sooner.

When I got a little bit older and saw what the priests had done to me, I backed away from believing there is a God because God would not allow that to go on. When I got older,

I saw the harm I had done to others and said, "Wow! It was not God. It was me who did those things."

When you take the fear away, that's the biggest thing that can happen to someone. Take away the fear of God. Some people go to their death bed and they are afraid of God. Why be afraid of the most loving, caring father in the history of the world or the planet? Why? Why be afraid of someone that is said to love you unconditionally? I was never afraid of God after that but I always despised those who represented him.

I started to think about other people giving me unconditional love – like Suzanne and my kids. When Suzanne came into my life, I started to realize what God was like. Before that, I did believe that God was around but it was never for me. Then I realized that God must be good if I'm still alive.

He must be good if I still have my kids. He must be good if I still have my wife. He must be good if I still have a family. Even though I'm not completely healthy, he must be good if I am healthy enough to at least do some things. I have to understand that at 75 I'm not the same person that I was at 60. I think that age has helped me in that respect.

I have more experience of life and more understanding of life. I have a better understanding that I don't need to be afraid, because I don't want the middle man. I know that I don't need a middle man. All my life I heard that God is the greatest thing in the world and then they told me to be afraid of him. How can I be afraid of the best person in the whole history of the planet?

I also realized that the evil was people against people.

I think I am getting closer to seeing a loving God.

Last year, when I was facing surgery – I called up a friend – he too was facing cancer warning. He said, "Rene, when I am afraid – especially before surgery or something like that, I just ask God to help me."

It sounded so simple – and I knew that this time I needed God's help.

I simply said, "Ask him for me?"

"I will, Rene."

Something happened to me at that moment.

Something changed.

CHAPTER TWENTY
Reflections

I still ask myself, "Why did I do that? Why didn't I choose a better path?"

I don't know why.

I just know that I ached for family. But I couldn't just get my family back, I had to survive. In order to live on the streets, to survive on the streets, I had to do certain things.

In those years I lacked opportunities. I lived in poverty. I didn't have any direction. I was street smart and had the skills to survive.

If I wanted money for supper, I had to find a way to get the money. I was only 14 or 15 and there aren't too many places to get work when you are that age. Who would hire me when I didn't have a place to live – an address?

I was living with a girl who was pregnant but it wasn't an address. It was basically a place to hide because I was only 14 and I was being very careful so that nobody could pick me up or arrest me. I did everything I could to push away anyone who was trying to be nice to me. I had a lack of trust and lack of understanding.

When I did have someone who cared, I pushed them away. It's as if I came to a point where I was on a path to self-destruction where I didn't want to trust anybody. I didn't want anybody around me. I didn't want to be manipulated by anybody. I didn't want to hear anybody talking to me about things I didn't want to hear. I was on a path to destruction.

I was a suicidal...I was self-destructive. Every day of my life I believe that after everything that happened when I was a kid, I've become a self-destructive person.

I wanted to die, I wanted to disappear, I wanted to feel nothing I was feeling. In my stomach, it was tense; I was like a time bomb. It was...living like this; I don't know how I managed to do this for so long.

But you become used to that, it becomes you. What you try to project at first, you become that animal, and when you are in the jungle, only the strongest animal survives. The rest, they die. Then for me, I will be the strongest animal they can ever see in this jail. They call me the crazy French man.

I always say the worst thing we can do to a kid is to put the kid in a rocking chair. You push, you push, you push, you push. Like a rocking chair... when you push back it will swing forward.

You'll never win that war. It's not possible because the kid doesn't know what the war is. He's just got the aggression coming out of here.

"Why is everybody against me? Why is everybody doing this?"

You ask those questions as a kid and you don't know the answers because the questions you ask, they're not even the right questions. You see this as people being against you, but it's not necessarily true because when you start to push and people don't understand, they push back. It's where they put the game for you to go down any path in life. It's the worst thing that cannot happen to a kid, the rocking chair.

When you keep doing things with that thought, how can you have time to forgive yourself? You don't. You have a life that explodes all over the place.

But I don't like the term "no choice." There are so many kids in our country who have been abused. There are kids who are beaten up every day by family members and they are able to put this in a different compartment than me and they survive like this. I cannot spend my life using this excuse, because other people did not all turn out to be robbers.

However, I put it into a compartment that turned everything into violence and aggression. I was aggressive as a kid. I always fought with the kids who were doing things to my brother. I was the guy who became the protector. I chased a guy with a skate because I was mad at him on the ice.

I have observed people all my life. You can't live the life of a robber, without being an observer. I was always watching people, following people, checking out what they were doing.

When I put my gun to the guy's head, I already knew every move he made when he was sitting in that truck because I had followed him for eight months prior to doing the job. We had started with a different truck, but it was the same run. It is just that company changed, because Brinks went on strike, but it was still the same run. This guy had been doing the route for two weeks.

You have to be an observer in the extreme when you do that kind of work. That is also why I was able to tell the teacher in the school where I was speaking, "You better watch that kid. He's going to end up in trouble." I knew right away, based on my observations. I was reliving my own life again.

These questions, and this guilt is something that will last as long as I'm alive.

I never achieved redemption. It is about trying to redeem yourself but never being finished.

How can you fill 30 years of crime with 20 years of good deeds here and there? Because even working for Life Line, I was getting paid to work for Life Line. For me it felt it wasn't enough.

It is crazy to put it this way. It is not payback -- it is owing. You always feel you owe something you can never pay back. For me it was never enough. If they called me to speak at five schools the same week, I would go to all five schools. Sometimes the United Way called me to do five speaking engagements on the same day, and I said yes. Because I did so much bad, how can you pay back? I live owing something to society and to everyone without ever paying back.

The hardest thing is to stop the hatred. You cannot really use the word love as long as you have the word hatred in your heart. And hatred never really left my heart. Even when I was in that line of work, it is as if my hatred was taking over the good. I had done so many things under the word hatred that I got love and hatred mixed up. It seems that hatred is the hardest one for me to deal with. I never get rid of hatred.

It was only when I met Wilma – and with all her questions that I put it together. I told her about the abuse when I was twelve years old. Then right after that we were speaking in a church together and it was the first time I used the term "sexually abused." I had never discussed it before with anyone in my life. Nobody…. And I did it with her. How can you take the hate if you don't discuss this for the last 40 years? Because if you don't talk about the hatred, you are going to always have it in your heart.

It is how I learned to deal with hatred…. And learning to love means you learn and then you falter, you learn and you falter…and so on….

Lots of people think that there is a right way to love and a bad way to love. That is nuts.

As a kid I always loved to listen to music that hurt. I loved to hear the hurt. There were lots of words I didn't understand in English, and it was always American or English music but the songs that were talking about pain, hatred, love were the ones I listened to. It was in that order. Pain, hatred, love. People who are not screwed up like I was – and still am – the order is love, pain, hatred. Because you disappear the other two. To me I have to empty my heart of hatred and anger if I really want to love.

For me, what I accomplished was never enough to get the forgiveness that I was after. And it is like the love you are after. You can never achieve the forgiveness you wish. You can never achieve the love that you want to…there is always more. There is a vulnerability in forgiveness and love.

Suzanne created weakness in me – created love. She created a really strong awareness, if I can use that term. People usually always love you to get something from you. Unconditional love is what she gave me, that's exactly what she gave me, as well as the children.

I kept on doing bad things over the years and she still loved me. Her commitment was way bigger than mine when we got married. I'm sure that if my commitment had been as strong as hers, I would not have robbed the Brinks truck.

Most of the time we always hurt the people we love the most. Forgiveness is for that….

Acknowledgements

I am eternally grateful to everyone who was a member of the village that supported me, encouraged me, and helped me change.

Special thanks to Alan Libman who helped create the Association in Defence of the Wrongly Convicted (AIDWYC).

Special thank you to my friends: Pierre Allard, Willie Gibbs, Dave Mills, Graham Reddoch, Art Makujt, Skip Graham, James Murphy, Drew Allen, Chris Price, Robert Bonnefoy.

Special thanks to Wilma Derksen for her work with victims of serious crime and her endless questions.

Special thanks to all the staff at Stony Mountain Institution who were so supportive of my work with Life Line.

My sincere apology and all my love to my wife Suzanne, my son's Daniel and Christian and to my daughter Melanie for the pain I put you through.

I would like to offer special thanks to John William Braithwaite who, although no longer with us, continues to inspire me and everyone who knew him.

JOHN WILLIAM BRAITHWAITE
MARCH 5, 1930 – JULY 4, 2019

John Braithwaite had an unforgettable impact on my life. I can't forget how important this man has been to me – like a father figure.

He impacted my life in every way, shape and form. He knew that I was doing everything to facilitate the life of my clients and he knew that I was passionate about Life Line.

Every time I met John, I felt, "Oh my god, I am going to meet John again!"

John was part of the Canada Criminal Justice Association and he is the only Canadian who was president of the American Correction Association. They voted for a Canadian! Can you imagine that? I can't believe how the people in the States respected him.

He was like a god within the American Correction Association. He helped them found the Association and even became the first president. They had so much respect for John. It only emphasized the respect I already had for him. John Braithwaite – the man who opened every door in the States for Life Line – our light – to the criminal justice system.

John was an icon in Corrections, a great man, a true friend and a mentor and inspiration to so many. He shone a searchlight on humane and progressive corrections. His optimism and his ability to get things done were an inspiration to everyone. Thank you, John.

PHOENIX AWARD GALA
By: Wilma Derksen

The Pierre Allard award evening was truly amazing evening.

First of all, as guests, we were guided down the long corridors of Stony Mountain Institution to the spacious lobby of the administration building which had been transformed into a ballroom.

There we mingled with about 50 guests who had flown in from across the country to attend this prestigious event, the Pierre Allard award given to only a very few select candidates worthy of the Phoenix Award.

The Phoenix, symbolizing rebirth, is an imaginary bird which according to ancient stories, burns itself to ashes every five hundred years and is then reborn. This mythical bird is multi-colored, a masterfully-combined medley of the most beautiful parts of all the birds in the world.

To describe someone or something as a phoenix means that they return again after being destroyed. It is beauty arising from ashes.

Mingling with this prestigious group of who's who in Corrections and hearing their praise of Rene and his work, all I could think of was my meeting with Willie Gibbs at the Congress 1995 of the Criminal Justice Association of Canada.

At that time, Gibbs was Senior Deputy Commissioner of the Correctional Service of Canada and then later he became the Chairman of the National Parole Board.

Gibbs approached me and told me that he had heard of my work with Rene and said that he had been warden of one of the prisons when Rene was an inmate.

Since I had heard Rene tell his story so often, I thought this was my opportunity to verify them.

I asked Gibbs, "Can you tell me what he was like?"

Gibbs grinned. "He was nasty… just nasty. He was probably the most dangerous inmate we had. He wasn't the usual convict. Because he wasn't a user and never did any drugs, he didn't need anything. There was nothing that we had to control him. He lived on anger – and hated everyone. He could fight – lie – and out-manipulate us all."

Gibbs shook his head as he remembered. "He truly operated only on hate."

"Do you think someone like that can change?" I asked.

"Yes, I do. I've seen it. I don't know how, but he did it. I do believe he has changed."

"Really?"

He nodded. "Yes, he's changed. I think we would know by now if he hadn't. There are a few of us here at the Congress who have experienced him as changed."

Rene - we celebrate your change.

*****

"Personal transformation can and does have global effects.

As we go, so goes the world, for the world is us.

The revolution that will save the world is ultimately a personal one." - Marianne Williamson

*****

Pardon

Government of Canada, Ottawa, Ontario, The National Parole Board is pleased hereby to award, Rene Charles Durocher a pardon under the Criminal Records Act.

And this pardon is evidence of the fact that the Board, after making proper inquiries was satisfied that the said, Rene Charles Durocher has remained free of any convictions since completing the sentence and was of good conduct and that the conviction(s) should no longer reflect adversely on his character and unless it ceases to exist or is subsequently revoked, requires the judicial record of conviction to be kept separate and apart from other criminal records and removes all disqualifications to which Rene Durocher is by reason of the conviction, subject by virtue of any Act of Parliament or a regulation made thereunder.

Given at Ottawa, this 21 day of March, 2007.

Signed, Mario Dion, chairperson.

Timeline

1943   Born September 17 Rene Charles Durocher in Lavaltrie, Quebec.

1961   Arrested - charged with possession of tools and sentenced 2 years in federal penitentiary.

> *He entered his first correctional institution at the age of 17 for an act of armed robbery. At the time, the Crown decided to try him as an adult to teach him a lesson.*

1963   Released from prison.

1964   Arrested for armed robbery, sentenced 14 years. Released on parole in May, 1971.

> *He had walked into a store while firing a newly purchased shotgun into the air.*

1971   Shoot out - arrested for armed robbery. His partner was killed.

1972   Sent to Archambault Maximum Security for 22 years. (25 years old)

1979   Sent to Stony Mountain Institution, Manitoba – met Suzanne.

1981   Parole Board approved full parole.

1982   Married Suzanne in Nelson, British Columbia.

Upon his third release from prison, he tried to lead a law-abiding life, but after several bad jobs and a failed business venture, Mr. Durocher found himself in financial difficulties, with a wife and two children to support. To correct the situation, he returned to what he knew best — crime — and participated in what was, at that time, the biggest robbery in Canadian history.

1985   Brinks truck robbery.

Rene and his partners robbed a Cache truck. He used the money from the robbery to buy a pet store.

1986   Arrested for $2 million Brink's truck heist in Montreal.

1987   Escaped to U.S.A. – "Most Wanted Man in Canada."

He surrendered to the Fifth Estate TV show three weeks later.

1987   Sent to Prince Albert Institution in Saskatchewan.

1988   Transferred to Stony Mountain Penitentiary in Manitoba.

It was only at this point in his life that Rene began to try to change himself. He worked with the prison psychologist at Stony Mountain Institution in Manitoba and learned to take responsibility for his crimes and to recognize the harm he had done to others.

1990   Warden Art Makujt invited Rene to apply for In-Reach worker position.

Upon his final release from prison, he committed himself to helping others and has since worked with agencies, such as Life Line, the John Howard Society of Manitoba, and the St. Leonard's Society, to assist inmates in turning their lives around.

1992   Rene meets Wilma Derksen at a school presentation.

1994   Rene became the national director of Life Line Canada.

1996   Rene and the Stony Mountain Lifers' group raise money for victims of serious crime.

1999   American Correction Association conference in the United States.

2006   Rene accepted executive director position at John Howard Society of Manitoba.

2007   Rene founded Manitoba Chapter of St. Leonard's Society of Canada.

2007   Rene received his pardon.

2008   Rene received the Pierre Allard Phoenix Award.

2010   Rene retires.

*****

It isn't a one, all-encompassing change. No, it cannot be one thing. It has to be a process. I followed a certain way of life for years and years and I could not change it with just one action. I went into prison when I was 17, and was in prison most of my life until I got out of prison when I was 47. When I look at a lifespan like that, there's not just one thing that caused this and there's not just one thing that will repair it. When I peel away my life, it's like peeling an onion. I'm sure there are lots of times I have forgotten what happened when I was peeling away the layers. There is lots of work to do because, my god, I'm talking about 30-some years in prison and much crime. - Rene Durocher